THE MAKING OF AN
IMMIGRATION JUDGE

THE MAKING OF AN
IMMIGRATION JUDGE

James Hanratty RD

QUARTET

First published in 2016 by Quartet Books Limited
A member of the Namara Group
27 Goodge Street, London W1T 2LD
Copyright © J. R. A. Hanratty 2016
The right of James Hanratty
to be identified as the author of this work
has been asserted by him in accordance with the
Copyright, Designs and Patents Act, 1988.
A catalogue record for this book
is available from the British Library
ISBN 9780704374126
Typeset by Josh Bryson
Printed and bound in Great Britain by
T J International Ltd, Padstow, Cornwall

To my wife, Pam

CONTENTS

FOREWORD
BY PETER HENNESSY

I first met James Hanratty when he invited me to speak at that great club of his, the Athenaeum, several years ago. From the moment we were introduced I knew him to be a man of passion, faiths and patriotism. This memoir reflects those qualities plentifully. Since then our friendship has blossomed and I have found James to be wonderfully gregarious company; he is certainly never boring and his intellectual curiosity ripples around the room.

James possesses zest, curiosity, optimism and an abundant sense of fairness – exactly the range of qualities and characteristics that are required of an immigration judge. It's a job for tough yet buoyant lawyers suffused with a generosity of spirit; all the woes of world and the scams of the world, too, pass through those court rooms in west London near Heathrow Airport.

James also wields a vivid pen. He makes the hidden wiring of Whitehall buzz. The way government departments work is undoubtedly an acquired taste and an arcane pursuit (which I happen to share), but anybody reading James's account of life in the Lord Chancellor's Department will be carried along because of his eye for episode, character and moment.

This book combines the big picture of serious questions facing the UK with the minute particulars, expressed with all the verve and insight you would expect from a man like James. His story of the case involving a Polish veteran of World War II, for example, is beautifully and movingly told – as are so many others within these pages.

Given the swirling arguments about immigration, migration, asylum and human rights which continue to disturb our national conversation, this is a book of timeliness and wisdom, and a welcome addition to that conversation. It is also a book of many bonuses. James's account of the last great British imperial handover – that of Hong Kong to China in 1997 – is vividly told from his position as both a participant and observer.

Throughout this book James is loyal and warm towards the many institutions that have shaped him – a very attractive characteristic. These institutions range from Stonyhurst College where he was schooled, to the Royal Naval Reserve, and the legal profession in many of its forms. It is fitting for a Jesuit-reared boy that he should finish with the great prayer of St Ignatius Loyola.

Peter Hennessy, Lord Hennessy of Nympsfield, FBA
Attlee Professor of Contemporary British History,
Queen Mary, University of London.

1

A DAY IN THE LIFE
OF AN IMMIGRATION JUDGE

The immigration judge struggled into work on a warm July morning from the nose to tail traffic on the M4. With classic bureaucratic incompetence, the court complex was situated under the Heathrow flightpath; the airport was just one mile away. When the jumbo jets jettisoned fuel over the car park, the complex became one of the most polluted places in Europe. Coughing mildly from the fumes, he wondered what was on his list; he always worried that he was not fully prepared.

The first case was a foreign criminal deportation appeal. A Sri Lankan man had injured someone with a cricket bat in a fight and been sentenced to fifteen months' imprisonment. The Home Office maintained that, as the sentence was over twelve months' imprisonment, deportation was automatic in law. The appellant, who was being detained after the completion of his sentence, was remorseful and wanted bail so he could return to his family. He also submitted that he could not be deported as he had a legitimate claim for asylum; he had supported the Tamil Tigers ten years previously and had torture marks on his leg from Sri Lankan soldiers. His human rights and his family life in the UK with his wife and child should also prevent deportation. The man had also recently realised, he submitted, that to a certain degree, he was gay.

An 'expert witness' on Sri Lanka from an obscure university in Wales supported his story, as did four further witnesses. The Home Office maintained in its refusal letter that he was probably not from Sri Lanka at all but Tamil Nadu in India. The medical report from a doctor was unreliable; the doctor had recently been criticised in the High Court for churning out similar reports. And the appellant was not gay at all. He could return to either India or Sri Lanka with

1

his family. The petition signed by 200 friends and neighbours was self-serving. The two sureties for bail were, according to the Home Office, unreliable. One was an impecunious Catholic priest who had visited the appellant in prison and the other an uncle from Penge. The smooth barrister representing the appellant had bushy sideburns carefully cultivated to give him a studied Dickensian appearance so he could bump up the brief fee he charged ignorant clients. He had just produced a 400 page background dossier on Sri Lanka submitted that morning.

The conscientious and experienced immigration judge sighed and looked at the other two cases. The first was from a Bangladeshi student who was still there and had been refused a visa to study at the East End College of Magnificence for a diploma in Tourist Studies. The entry clearance officer had submitted that the college was a 'dodgy' one and that Bangladesh had no tourist industry. The third case consisted of a Kenyan headmaster of a leading school in Nairobi who wished urgently to visit his dying grandfather in Birmingham. The entry clearance officer in Nairobi submitted that this man would not return to Kenya after the visit but would become an illegal mini-cab driver in Slough, just like his cousin.

The judge, who by now was not amused at the length of the list, phoned the listing officer to ask for an explanation. He was told a senior judge had approved the list to try to improve the tribunal daily disposal rate! The judge would sit alone for the bail hearing and for the two smaller cases but would sit with a lay member on the deportation case. The lay member breezed in at 9.30 a.m. not having had time to read the papers. He had been an executive for the Milk Marketing Board but when told the asylum case was from Sri Lanka, said he had once been on holiday to Ceylon – as he insisted on calling it – many years previously. He questioned whether the off spinner Muttiah Muralitharan had a 'legitimate bowling action.'

Then the usher arrived, a cheerful cockney lady with a smoker's cough, to announce that the air conditioning had broken down in the courtroom and the staff had refused to open the first floor window for security reasons. It was at that point the judge made his first three decisions of the day. Number one was to order the six-foot-seven security officer, a former Pashtun warrior in an ill-fitting uniform, to open the window, the second was to hear the Kenyan case first and the third was to make himself a strong cup of coffee.

These cases were typical but fictional for the purpose of this story. I was such a judge for sixteen years, trying to be patient and kind but also firm and wise and up to date with the complex and ever changing domestic and international law. I, too, was urged to hear more cases in the day to increase the disposal rate. My nature was naturally compassionate, yet I was acutely aware of the many immigration rackets. I knew – and the appellants knew – that my job was to try as carefully as I could to decide who was telling the truth and who was lying. At times it was a very demanding task.

So how did I get there? How was I, of all people, fitted to carry out the judicial task so vital to others, possibly with a risk to life or destruction of a family or indeed serious risk to the general public if the decision, one way or the other, in lengthy judgments, was wrong? It all started back in 1946.

2
EARLY BEGINNINGS

I had to be eligible to play cricket for Yorkshire, so early in 1946 my father, a proud Yorkshireman, then still in the Royal Navy, drove my pregnant mother from the Royal Marines Barracks in Deal all the way to Leeds in an ancient Austin 7. I was born in Leeds on 6 February 1946. I never played for Yorkshire.

My father came from a long line of Irish landowners. His father had come to England in 1910 as a doctor, while his uncle served with the Grenadier Guards as a doctor in World War I. After being educated at Stonyhurst College in Lancashire and qualifying from medical school, my father joined the Royal Navy early in 1943 and served on board HMS *Cam* on the North Atlantic and other convoys. He was often the only doctor in a squadron of six frigates.

Naturally, my father had many stories from his seafaring days. He was on board HMS *Cam* on D-Day off the French coast when an able seaman came to see him complaining of a vicious stomach ache. My father immediately diagnosed acute appendicitis and asked the captain to return to Falmouth at once in order to save this seaman's life. The captain, a brave Royal Naval Reserve (RNR) officer with a Distinguished Service Cross, told my father the ship could not leave station. My father was informed he had half an hour to sort out the problem during which time the ship would slow down to mitigate the effects of a Force 6 wind and choppy seas.

The seaman was laid out on the wardroom table like a flat kipper and the first lieutenant administered gas while a nervous orderly provided support. Before my father could make the initial incision the first lieutenant had already fainted. My father's first incision, he told me later, nearly castrated the poor seaman as he made it at the very moment the ship hit an enormous wave. Nevertheless, the appendix was removed. The life of the seaman was saved. My father and the seaman corresponded for decades afterwards. Indeed, at my father's funeral, early in 2014, I mentioned this story at the end of my eulogy. In order to provide the proof, I proclaimed, 'In case anyone does not believe me, here is the appendix of that lucky seaman,' and held up the appendix, to gasps of surprise. We had found it in a medicine bottle after my father died.

Late in 1944 HMS *Cam* was severely damaged after she mistakenly dropped a depth charge on a sunken ammunition ship; forty-nine crew were injured, some seriously. My father not only had to see to the injured, he had to take command of the stricken vessel. Later he was Mentioned in Despatches for his leadership and medical competence.

My parents met at the Royal Marine Barracks in Deal where my father had been transferred after HMS Cam had been written off. My mother had moved there from the Naval Hospital at Haslar in Portsmouth. She was a sister in Queen Alexandra's Royal Naval Nursing Service (QARNNS). She herself came from a most interesting family. Her father, my grandfather, was Andrew Belton who should have been more widely known as an early adventurer. He flew with the Wright Brothers in Chicago, put down a rebellion on behalf of the King of Morocco and was made a general in the Moroccan Army before World War I. Later, he was a fighter pilot with the Royal Flying Corps during World War I with several kills to his name before he was gassed. His wife, whom I never knew, was Marie Babin, a French Canadian opera singer who sang at the Metropolitan Opera of New York and the Albert Hall. She was descended from Captain La Foret sent to 'New France' by Louis XIV. They were married in 1913.

My grandmother on my mother's side died in 1936 of pneumonia aged only forty-six. My grandfather abandoned my mother, then aged sixteen, with his sister and her husband, a Wykehamist and past master of the Skinners Company, in their house in Onslow Square, London where she resided for several years.

Later, my mother attended Queen's Secretarial College and was posted to the Middlesex Hospital. Here she realised her true vocation lay in nursing. So she transferred to the nursing team in Middlesex Hospital, which in those days was a singularly exclusive body of competent and usually well-born women. At the beginning of the war she joined QARNNS and nursed the great captain Johnny Walker in Liverpool before he died of a cerebral haemorrhage resulting from exhaustion. Both my parents were very proud of their naval background.

My father had been offered the best medical practice in Cowes in the Isle of Wight from the senior partner who was dying. The deal was made but then my father had his demobilisation from the Royal Navy postponed for six months; he had to remain in the service to care for the returning British prisoners of war from the Far East with significant and appalling injuries and illnesses. Unfortunately, the deal to take over this practice in Cowes fell through. Later, my father found a practice in Derbyshire near Chesterfield where he practised as senior partner for just over thirty years.

Much later, my father was headhunted to be the medical director of St Joseph's Hospice in London, the largest in the world. He became a pioneer of hospice care and helped Dame Cicely Saunders to introduce the 'syringe driver' to supply continuous pain killers. He was the author of two text books and tutored doctors from all over the world in hospice care. He was eventually awarded the OBE. In my view he deserved far more. He was elected to the Athenaeum, the distinguished club for academics, in Pall Mall, London. As his obituary in *The Times* observed, he was 'the unsung hero of the hospice movement.'

So my parents settled in Derbyshire and became prominent in ex-service circles. He became the president of the local British Legion. He was eventually elected chairman of the Derbyshire BMA. His practice was noted for the particularly high standard of medicine practised there. Both my parents had that strength of character forged by war, which meant they just knew, instinctively, how to cope. My father once cut his leg wide open with a powered hedge cutter. He put ten stitches into his own leg without fuss.

My mother was strong and also widely read and cultured, a keen amateur historian. She could be strict with us. When school report time came she would say, 'Your father will see you now in his study.' This was a bad sign.

My sister Mary was born in 1947, brother John in 1949, Patrick in 1952 and Peter in 1957. They all had successful careers. Mary was a nurse like her mother at the Middlesex Hospital and married a distinguished architect. Patrick, John and Peter all joined financial institutions and did well in the City. Patrick and Peter later established an enormous plantation in Madagascar growing bio diesel fuels and peppers, employing 1,000 workers at decent rates of pay.

My parents were Roman Catholics so I was despatched to the local church to be a young altar boy aged six but this didn't last long. One Whit Sunday when lighting the candles on the altar I managed to set fire to a large bunch of flowers hovering over the flames like butterflies. Panic. In an embarrassing display of unwanted heroism, a member of the congregation threw water from a flower pot over the flames and me. There was great consternation all round.

At the age of five I was sent to St Joseph's Convent, a day school in Chesterfield. My sister, Mary, followed me there a year later. Being rather cleverer than me she joined my class despite being a year younger. The education there was sound with fine teaching. The nuns had taken in some orphans who lived with them but were educated free of charge. I became very friendly with two of them, Ross and Barry, and often invited them back to our house for weekends. I still remember the look of awe on their faces when they saw our large house standing proudly in several acres. We had plenty of land, a cricket pitch, a croquet lawn and a tennis court.

These two boys, whom I still remember well, made me acutely aware of how fortunate I was.

My father had been educated by the Jesuits at Stonyhurst College in Lancashire and wanted to send me there too. Consequently, at the age of eight I was despatched to the prep school for an interview with the headmaster, Father Fishwick. All was going well as I remembered that Alfred, King of Wessex, had burned the cakes. But I was then asked what six multiplied by nought was. I insisted that the answer was six. Nevertheless, I was accepted and started there in 1954. The day I left home I wanted to take my teddy bear but my father refused, saying I was a man now. When I entered the dormitory I saw that every boy had his own teddy bear from home. I cried myself to sleep. I can still visualise that ginger bear now.

In those days there were no exeats, no weekends at home and no half terms. I saw my parents for three hours twice a term when they came to visit to take me out to lunch. When tea time arrived, I had that sinking feeling in the base of my stomach as I knew I would soon be returning to school and my parents would leave me there. Those visits were actually deeply upsetting. This went on for nine months in the year. Fifty years later I told my mother, only half humorously, that I regarded this treatment as inhumane and contrary to Article 3 of the European Convention on Human Rights, which I was by then well used to applying from the bench. She replied by saying that on my first day, after they had said goodbye, she had to step out of the car two miles down the road to be physically sick. It had taken her fifty years to mention that; fifty years where I thought I had just been dumped far away.

During the holidays, especially during the summer, I would watch county cricket and go to many parties of family friends, all from a similar, mostly wartime background. It was an uncomplicated life. At the age of eleven at the Stonyhurst prep school I was most lucky enough to be educated for a year by Father Ernest Clarke. He was so brilliant the local authority in Lancashire used to bring the occasional group of young teachers to watch him at work. At the age of eleven I could easily have passed the GCSE or O-level, as it was called then, in Latin, so inspired was his teaching. He had the right to order us to be beaten for misdemeanours but never did. He never had to. He had the light and human touch. Once, when it was snowing and we were all staring out of the window, he saw how distracted we were and allowed us to get up and look out of the beautiful bow windows for three minutes at this magical, gentle, fluffy powder, before we returned to Hillard and Botting's Latin Primer.

In my last year I was made third head of the school with some responsibilities, mainly in organising games. Soon after, I passed into St Mary's Hall, the intermediate school for Stonyhurst, and was placed in a class headed by the worst kind of embittered Irish priest whose main method of educating was to organise the beating of the boys. Fortunately, there was a grading exam in order to put boys into the class according to their ability. I worked hard and passed the exam well enough to be moved upwards and away from this dreadful man. In the summer we took the common entrance exam to gain entry into Stonyhurst; there were a surprising number of failures as the standards were pretty high.

I had passed the exam in May, meaning there was little more to do for the remainder of the summer term than play cricket in glorious sunshine and enjoy picnics down by the River Hodder. At St Mary's Hall I was awarded my cricket colours for taking five wickets for five runs against a school called Hale Barns. I also learnt a lesson when a master bet me sixpence I couldn't hit a six over mid-wicket from a ball bowled by a boy called Bullen. Needless to say, I swiped with my head held high, missed the ball and was clean bowled, a lesson for life. The master waived the right to his sixpence.

When I passed into Stonyhurst College it was totally different from the friendly and cosy existence at the prep schools. The place was vast. It was unlike most public schools in that everyone was under one roof; the building was reputed to be the largest in the country, under one roof, except for Hampton Court Palace. The building had been gifted to the Jesuits by Thomas Weld of Lulworth in 1793. A direct descendant was Joseph Weld who learned the basics of yacht design at Stonyhurst. He was a founder member of the Royal Yacht Squadron in 1815, which I joined nearly 200 years later.

The education I received at Stonyhurst was tightly disciplined but we were all encouraged to think for ourselves. Unlike the impression of people who are not Catholics, the Jesuits there were not scheming and Machiavellian at all but were men of considerable intellectual ability and wide experience from around the world. They included renowned scientists, astronomers, linguists and theologians. Several of them had been decorated for bravery in World War II as soldiers. Religion was not forced into us. We could make up our own minds. Nevertheless, some of the religious experiences there still linger in the memory. The first High Mass of the year was always Kitson in D, including the most beautiful Kyrie I have ever heard. The bases would start, then the tenors, then the altos and finally the trebles, including me, in soaring music to the glory of God.

The college itself had a fine reputation for discipline and loyalty to the crown. The impressive war memorial showed the vast number of boys who had been killed in the two world wars and other conflicts. Seven old boys of the college have won the Victoria Cross (VC), including Maurice Dease who won the first VC of World War I at Mons. Their portraits are displayed proudly on the wall in the magnificent Elizabethan refectory.

Years later, in 2013, when I was president of the Stonyhurst Association, I had the honour of laying a wreath at the Menin Gate in Ypres honouring the thousands who had no known grave. After the ceremony I glanced up at the names engraved on the high stone walls. It was extraordinary and deeply moving as the first one I saw was G. Archer-Shee. He was the eponymous hero of Terence Rattigan's play *The Winslow Boy*, about a lad who was accused of stealing a postal order at the Naval College at Osborne. He was acquitted to great national rejoicing after an expensive defence paid for by his father. He was sent to Stonyhurst and, naturally, could not join the Royal Navy in World War I. Subsequently, he joined the Staffordshire Regiment with the son of the KC who had represented him. Both were killed at Ypres in 1914.

This has stayed with me over the years because my father often used the example of when the father in the play asked the boy whether he had stolen the postal order. The boy looked his father in the eye and swore his innocence. That word was good enough for the father. My father always said he would back us to the hilt provided we always told him the truth. We always did as we had a huge respect for him.

The Combined Cadet Force at Stonyhurst was compulsory for the whole school. I remember with amazement taking part in the Advance in Review Order where 400 cadets marched forward fifteen paces and stopped without a command. This was done in front of an astonished and rather inebriated inspecting general who could not believe what he had seen. Many of my school friends joined the Army or the Royal Marines and had successful careers. There was also a tradition of boys going into law and several of my colleagues became judges. There were prominent surgeons among them too. The classical education was very highly regarded and a stream of boys went off to Oxbridge each year to read classics.

Nevertheless, corporal punishment, did take place. When deemed necessary, the boys were beaten on the hands with an unforgiving piece of rubber known as a ferula. But the college had the tradition that when this punishment was ordered by a master, that particular master could not administer it, perhaps in a simmering temper. The boy, therefore, had to go elsewhere to receive this rather unpleasant experience. Sometimes it was ordered where perhaps it should not have been.

I remember I was not particularly good at physics and could not remember what Ohm's Law was. I was ordered to be beaten.

Yet, when the O-level came round I still could not remember it. Many years later in the Athenaeum, which generously elected me in 1996, there was a debate about corporal punishment. I got up and remarked that I was living proof that corporal punishment doesn't work because I was beaten to remember Ohm's Law and yet could not remember it subsequently in the exam. By one of the most astonishing coincidences, the very same physics master who had ordered this punishment, and who had since became a headmaster elsewhere, was among the audience. He could hardly wait to commiserate after dinner and inspect my once sore hands!

The education at Stonyhurst encouraged public speaking and debating. I was fortunate to win the prize debate with the motion 'This House would have peace at any price'. I spoke against the motion and my prize at the school speech day was to receive the memoirs of Field Marshal Lord Montgomery. Inside the front cover was written that I had won this prize for 'Ars Disputandi'!

I also entered the elocution competition regularly. But much to my dismay, Roderick Strange, later the Monsignor in charge of Beda College in Rome, would recite about ten minutes of Cicero in Latin. I would recite some Shakespeare like Henry V berating the Dauphin for the gift of tennis balls. So Roddy always won. I usually came second. Sadly, there was no prize for second.

I acted often on the well-equipped stage in the academy room. I was Sergeant Mitchem in *The Long and the Short and the Tall* by Willis Hall. The reviewer in the *Stonyhurst Magazine* wrote that, 'Hanratty started out with a rich Geordie accent. Unfortunately this accent moved steadily south-west during the course of the performance!'

I also learned to deal with injustice, which was useful for my career as a judge. In front of the college were two beautiful ponds 200 yards long. They would often freeze over during the winter so we could ice skate on them. One day I fell over and hit my head on the ice and acquired a black eye. I was then hauled before a rather severe priest who asked me in typical Jesuit fashion, 'With whom were you fighting and when?' I replied I had fallen on the ice and that this had caused my black eye. Subsequently, I was accused of being mendacious, which I remember thinking a long word at the time. He ordered me to be beaten, just three times, for my deceit. Fortunately I had a sense of humour. But I remembered the feeling of injustice and decades later on the bench I always tried to ensure that everyone in court left with the knowledge that the hearing had been a fair one.

The standard of school rugby was very high and the first XV were heroes. They were allowed extra meat and a Guinness during lunch in order to bulk themselves up. One year the first XV won every single match against many leading school sides. There were two boys who subsequently became internationals, Barry O'Driscoll who played for Ireland and Nick Drake-Lee who played for England. Many of the rest of the team became county players. But I only gravitated as far as the third XV known affectionately as 'The Turds.' One day we challenged the second XV to a match. It was one of the most violent and bloody I have ever witnessed or taken part in. And we beat them. I scored a try; and I remember the side step to this day.

We would go to schools like Rossall, on the bleak Lancashire coastline with gale force sleet skimming straight off the Irish Sea, to play on their freezing rugby pitches in February. Often we were roundly slaughtered by boys who always seemed rather larger than us.

But my abiding interest was, of course, cricket. I played for hours and hours and often neglected my studies. I managed to reach the first XI on the basis that I tried to emulate Gary Sobers. I bowled left arm medium pace over the wicket, left arm round the wicket spinners and left arm over the wicket chinaman, which is the left handers wrist spin; it is an off break to a right-handed batsman. The great coach, Jim Smith, from Middlesex and England would watch me and eventually observed to the captain, 'He will do.' So I played in the first XI, though I never really distinguished myself there. I remember being hit for six at Sedbergh and over cover point too. I was rebuked by my captain for congratulating the gifted batsman on a superb shot!

In those days I had a rather strong temper, probably passed down from my Irish ancestry, particularly around the age of fourteen. We used to go into the woods by the River Hodder near a place called 'The Thirty-Nine Steps' after the John Buchan novel. This was near the college and was part of the estate of three thousand acres owned by Stonyhurst College. One time we were to play a 'wide game'. This was very simple. It consisted of two flags on either side of a muddy valley and the object was that a rugby ball should be placed at the foot of the opposing flag. This involved climbing up a steep muddy slope in a scrum formation. I was captain of one of these teams. We were about a foot away from the opposing flag with our rugby ball when the tough priest from Glasgow, who was watching avidly, kicked the ball down to the bottom of the valley. I accused him of cheating and with flailing, small fists attacked him for spoiling our assured victory.

My father then received a formal letter from the college virtually accusing me of sacrilege; I had attacked a priest and was liable to be excommunicated and certainly expelled. When I explained the circumstances to my father he backed me up and replied that of course, although I had attacked a priest, I had not been attacking him because he was a priest but because he was a cheat who had spoiled an afternoon's fun. My father then added that if his son were to be expelled all his other sons would automatically be withdrawn from the college as well and sent to Ampleforth College. Faced with the prospect of all these school fees being lost – and gained by the Benedictines of Ampleforth – the college bursar and headmaster swiftly raised the white flag and backed down. This was a good example of the 'Winslow Boy' relationship I had with my father.

I made very close friends at the college. Some of us, aged fifteen, built a shelter on Longridge Fell made of wood covered with turf rather like an early Anglo Saxon settlement. In this we lit fires and cooked baked beans and delicious sizzling sausages in melted butter. It was then I had my only experience of smoking cigarettes. I smoked three but like President Clinton, I did not inhale! I suffered such terrible stomach cramps that I never smoked another cigarette ever again.

O-levels came and went. I passed a sufficient number well enough to move on to A-Levels. Notwithstanding the long hours idly playing cricket, I was offered a place at Nottingham University to study History. I had attempted to gain entry into Liverpool University to read history. When I was called for interview in Liverpool I turned up with my best college Sunday suit, hair neatly parted and a hideous spot on my chin. The senior lecturer asked me about the English Civil War so I told him that Lord Mohun had field guns and explained the battles including Naseby and Preston. I spoke of the perceived divine right of kings. I deplored the puritanism of Cromwell whose statue in Westminster is deliberately outside Parliament because he raided it. I mentioned the skill and discipline of the New Model Army but decried the later slaughter in Ireland. Alas, only when it was far too late did I notice the thin, bloodless lips, twitching mouth, humourless face and bright red socks of the interviewer, a born roundhead. I received the rejection in three days, the swiftest then ever recorded!

I left Stonyhurst feeling rather sad and I remain drawn to the place, partly owing to the beauty of its unspoilt location, the memories and a lingering feeling that I should have made more of my opportunities there.

3

FIRST STEPS IN THE LAW

Just as I was about to move to Nottingham to start studying history I found, to my horror, that this course was not an examination of European history in the eighteenth and nineteenth centuries but an exercise in translating Beowulf from the Anglo Saxon into English. I realised this was way beyond my intellectual abilities and would lead nowhere. All I might do with my degree, should I ever finish it, would be to become a disgruntled history teacher, a Mr Chips in some minor prep school wearing a tweed jacket with leather patches. I would coach cricket and eventually marry the matron. With this in mind I tried to transfer to law but the university quite rightly refused. I was too late.

Accordingly, I went down to the Law Society, the professional body of solicitors in London, for an interview and to ask advice of senior officials there. They recognised me for what I was, a public schoolboy with a sense of entitlement who needed some tough treatment to realise that success had to be earned. They recommended I did not go to university but did five years' articles, a form of apprenticeship, in a firm in Derbyshire. So I undertook this and it was just the sort of experience that at that time I needed.

I soon discovered that some of my friends at university were mainly playing table football in the local pub and drinking very seriously. They were not really doing very much studying at all, except in the days before exams. I joined the Sheffield Law Students Society and travelled round the country on moots, a form of law debate, at places like Southampton University. My school debating experience turned out to be very useful.

The solicitors' practice I joined included litigation and I used to listen in awe to the local county court judge, His Honour Judge

Sunderland, give the most learned and erudite judgments in running down road accident cases. I marvelled at the way evidence was marshalled, facts clearly found, the law applied and a fair decision made. His organised approach was a model for me to follow on the bench thirty years later. At the same time, I found conveyancing a bore. I was almost negligent at it. Indeed, on one occasion when conveyancing for a house builder I nearly conveyed all the houses to the buyers on the wrong side of the street.

One of my jobs as a junior articled clerk had been to serve writs on those who failed to keep up with their mortgage payments and were to be evicted from their houses. Many of these people were coal mining families where the miner had bought his first house, had been working to exhaustion to make the payments and then became injured. As a result, he was unable to repay the mortgage on time. I formed a very considerable respect for the coal mining community to whom my father would lecture on Saturdays in first aid. He would go down the mines with their very dirty, narrow tunnels to treat injured miners. On at least one occasion he had to do an amputation hundreds of feet down in a dusty ill-lit pit. Their courage was immense. Nearly all of them wished there was some other life besides the one of descending down the pit, with its risk of injury and the certainty of permanent lung damage.

Occasionally, I would turn up at a miner's house, serve the writ on the embarrassed husband and wife and then invite myself in for tea. I would explain to them how they could avoid eviction by coming to a settlement with the building society to give them more time to pay. I was not being disloyal to my client, a large national building society which had better remain unnamed. I was merely helping the building society avoid litigation and further expense by finding a way to secure a resumption of regular payments. This experience of articles helped me to recognise that the law should be synonymous with justice when sometimes it is not. Years later I would announce in court that I was in the 'justice business'.

I also studied at the Birmingham College of Commerce with its trail-blazing courses in practical litigation. My flat, which I shared with other law students, was right in the middle of several nurses' homes. This enabled me to learn the facts of life rather late but in a practical manner! I took one nurse to see and hear Manitas de Plata, the most amazing and talented guitarist ever.

Soon after, I joined the College of Law in Guildford to do a six month course in order to take the part one of the Solicitors Finals. I passed them without too much difficulty. Surprisingly, I got a distinction in that driest of subjects, land law. I enjoyed my time in Guildford and regularly lunched in the Ship Inn near the College of Law. I remember devouring hundreds of scotch eggs on the basis someone told me that they would cause a hairy chest. This was only partially successful.

After another period of articles in which I had more responsibility, I returned to the College of Law in Guildford to do part two of the exams, the finals, which were at that time regarded as perhaps the most difficult and demanding exams of any professional body. We had sixty people in our class. On the first day the lecturer said that only twenty-five per cent of us would pass and so we should make sure we were in the top twenty-five per cent in the mocks. I was surrounded by people who had got double firsts at Oxbridge in law so I wondered where I was going to feature in all this. I worked extremely hard and limited my social life to Saturday nights only when I sometimes worked as a disk jockey at parties. Once I played Serge Gainsbourg and Jane Birkin's 'Je t'aime' four times running as the dancers were so glued together in the middle of the dimly lit dance floor. The rest of the time I stayed in and worked. I persuaded myself to write off six months of my life just to pass these exams.

The exams in Alexandra Palace in north London were thoroughly intimidating. For one cold week in February it would be filled with 2,000 desks with inadequate heating and pigeons flying around the roof depositing their mess on unsuspecting students and their exam papers. Some students were unsure which to protect, their papers or themselves. When the revenue law exam took place and the command was given that we may open our papers from a man with a greying moustache and greasy black hair, there was a deafening crash behind me. I looked to find a grey-haired man, aged about forty-five, who had just fainted. I felt so sorry for him because I deduced that he could have been a retired army officer embarking on a second career with children and a mortgage. Suddenly, he had realised that he was not going to pass the exam with all the financial and other consequences that this would entail. He was carried out pale and unconscious on a stretcher.

Later, in the equity and succession exam, an elegant student wearing a cravat with a smart blazer who had been to Oxford walked formally down the centre aisle and bowed before the main invigilator. Arrogantly, he held up his exam paper and slowly tore it into tiny pieces and cast them into the air. He received a rippling round of applause. He had made his point and then stalked out. Even I could see that, although he had had his moment of fame, he certainly had not passed the exam.

I passed all the exams except commercial law. I could never work out who was liable in cases where frozen strawberries were being sent from Liverpool, with a German crew, in a British owned vessel to the Far East when the refrigeration had broken down in Aden and all the strawberries ruined before the buyer could receive them. This was all to do with the Sale of Goods Act and where ownership had actually passed from one to another. I seemed to get this spectacularly wrong.

So I went to the College of Law at Lancaster Gate to do a revision course in commercial law led by the extrovert Robert Lowe. Lowe would produce problems and stride down the class room to ask some cowering student what the answer was by saying to the student that he was 'too clever by….' When the student in fright eventually muttered 'half', Lowe would applaud as the student had got the right answer. He was so brilliant that I sailed through the exam and found myself qualified as a solicitor in December 1970.

I received my certificate at a formal ceremony at the Law Society with my proud parents in attendance. Even my friends came and applauded.

After all that, I wasn't sure what to do next. I wasn't attracted to private practice. Fortunately, I managed to engineer an interview with Dick Thompson, the registrar in the Criminal Appeal Office at the Royal Courts of Justice. The office was, and still is, responsible for servicing the professional needs of the Lords Justices of Appeal hearing appeals from the Crown Court. Thompson was a remarkable man, slightly eccentric, with a daughter who was an internationally recognised saxophone player. He was a brilliant mathematician who had risen to the rank of lieutenant colonel in the Royal Signals in World War II. He had a distinguished war record. I was interviewed by him and we got on famously as I was well prepared. He invited me to join the legal team there, at first on probation.

I found myself in a group of lawyers, many of whom were ex-service lawyers including an air commodore in the RAF legal services. I soon deduced this particular individual was gay in a Noel Coward kind of way. He was tall and elegant with perfectly manicured fingers and nails and he always wore a black jacket and pin-striped trousers. He was very amusing in conversation. Very early on I was invited to join him for an evening at the Royal Festival Hall and for dinner afterwards. I was pretty naïve in those days and accepted. We enjoyed a fine concert and then we adjourned to a restaurant in Charlotte Street. Half way through dinner he remarked dryly to me how many nephews were there with their uncles. So I looked around and realised there was not a single female in the entire place. But I still did not click.

He then invited me back to his flat in Hallam Street for a coffee and I accepted. It was only when he emerged from the bedroom wearing an elegant flowing Chinese silk dressing gown and smelling of Aramis perfume that I realised I had been invited there for something other than witty conversation. I stood up in a panic, looked at my watch, announced my last Tube train was about to leave and rushed out. The next day he invited me in for a chat in his office and said he had thoroughly enjoyed the previous evening but would be awfully grateful if I would not mention this to anyone else. I gave him my promise. He was a kind and amusing man who died many years ago.

The work in the Criminal Appeal Office was really interesting. As a lawyer there you had to summarise the case which had been heard at the Crown Court with constant references to the particular transcript. Then you would point out the law which had to be applied but, of course, as the lawyer advising the Lords Justices of Appeal you could not say how the case should be decided or how the law should be applied; that was matter for the Lords Justices. We were merely there to give guidance.

I would sit in court as a registrar with wig and gown on to run the proceedings. I had my moments. One day a Methodist minister in a dog collar appeared as a witness. When I asked him in standard fashion whether he wished to swear on the Bible or affirm, he replied that he wished to affirm. So without any hesitation I recited the mantra, 'Do you wish to affirm because you have no religious beliefs or because taking the oath is contrary to any religious beliefs that you do have?' The judges giggled. The Methodist minister then decided he would swear on the Bible after all.

On another occasion I was registrar in court with a tough panel of Lord Justice Lawton in the middle and Mr Justice Melford Stevenson and Mr Justice Chapman on either side. This was a formidable triumvirate. In those days breathalyser cases could reach the Court of Appeal because they were heard in the Crown Court. Now they are heard in magistrates' courts and it is rare that any such case would ever reach the Court of Appeal. A very earnest and nervous looking barrister from Manchester with a very strong northern accent came down to conduct the appeal. He stood up trembling in front of this panel of judges and proclaimed, 'My Lords this case is very simple. The provisions of the Road Safety

Act provide that it is an offence to drive a motor vehicle on a road while exceeding the prescribed blood alcohol limit. Well,' he said triumphantly, 'my client was well over the limit but at the time of the accident he was not on a road at all but on a footpath before he drove into several people in a bus queue. Accordingly he did not contravene the provisions of the Road Safety Act as he was not on a road.' There was a stunned silence in court as his argument was clearly both moral and legal nonsense.

Eventually, there was the sound of a copy of *Archbold: Criminal Pleading, Evidence and Practice* being slammed shut and a rustle of the green curtains behind the Lords Justices. I peered behind me to see Mr Justice Melford Stevenson storming out of the court room. Lord Justice Lawton and Mr Justice Chapman then had a quiet conversation and the large and formidable Chapman stood up, swept through the curtains and bellowed down the corridor, 'Melford, Melford, Fred says you've got to come back!' So Mr Justice Melford Stevenson reappeared. For the next forty minutes I heard the most magnificent diatribe from all three judges as they took this wretched little barrister from Manchester slowly apart. The appeal was unsuccessful. The barrister went on to pastures new outside the law.

During this time I also had an experience that made me worry constantly about the consequences of my actions. There had been a murder case at the Old Bailey. The defendant had returned early from work to find his wife in bed with another man. He then proceeded to shoot this man with a shotgun and attempted to murder his wife, who survived. The trial at the Old Bailey was presided over by a High Court judge who told the jury, 'Members of the jury you must be reasonably sure of the facts before you can convict.' That word 'reasonably' was contrary to law. He had misdirected the jury. I noted this in reading the transcript although this had not been picked up by the barrister in charge of the appeal of this appellant.

Afterwards, I consulted Dick Thompson. He recognised the gravity at once and told me to go to see Lord Justice Patrick

O'Connor and take advice. I called on Lord Justice O'Connor and explained the situation to him. He immediately granted leave to appeal to this man. The appeal was heard before the Lord Chief Justice Widgery and two Lords Justices. The Old Bailey sent their most distinguished prosecuting barristers to lead for the prosecution. But the Lord Chief Justice said to them, 'Well I don't think there is anything we can do.' The appeal was conceded. This appellant was then released and announced as he left court that he was now going to try to find his separated wife and 'do her too'. He was promptly rearrested but was released on the order of another judge at the Old Bailey. As far as I know, fortunately, he never found his wife. It troubled me for a long time afterwards; although I had got the law right I felt somehow I may have been responsible for a miscarriage of justice.

At this time I shared an office with Eric Blandford who had been a High Court judge in the colonial service and was a very good practical lawyer. I was with him for two years and he taught me the correct way to interpret legislation in order to become learned in the law. When I moved on after two years I presented him with a silver dish from the Silver Vaults in Chancery Lane. This tough old lawyer was moved to tears.

I remained always most respectful and full of admiration for the ability of the Lord Justices of Appeal whom I served. These included people like Lord Justice Lawton, Fenton Atkinson and Sachs, O'Connor and Roskill, Edmund Davies and Scarman. The last three went up to the House of Lords. Lord Justice Lawton kindly persuaded Lord Justice Roskill to be my referee for further advancement.

A favourite Lord Justice of mine was John Megaw from Northern Ireland. He had played rugby for Ireland in the second row and was formidable physically and intellectually. But he was never keen on wading through reams of papers in hopeless cases; one day he stormed into court to announce that the transcripts weighed seventeen pounds on the bathroom scales. That was not as amusing as the image of him staggering upstairs carrying these transcripts, dumping them on the bathroom scales and, in triumph, declaring to his patient and long-suffering wife that they weighed seventeen pounds. However, in meritorious cases he was assiduous, careful, learned and right. I miss the great John Megaw.

I suppose my lucky break came when, one day, I was in court as registrar during a discussion on the sentence tariff for supplying cannabis, then a fairly new offence. I rose to say to the presiding Lord Justice Edmund Davies that by the following morning I would have a schedule of previous cases for the court, the counsel and solicitors. Somewhat surprised by my gusto, Davies LJ adjourned. I rushed out of court, grabbed the main typist and asked her if, for a large box of chocolates, she could be in by 7 a.m. the following morning. Intrigued, she agreed. There was no internet or computers then; case records were held on cards in shoe boxes. So I spent most of the night wading through the boxes and old files. With the help of this chocolate loving typist, by 9.30 a.m. each judge, solicitor and counsel had received a schedule showing the name, number, facts and sentence for every trial and the appeal and comments. There were fifteen such cases. Edmund Davies was effusive with his thanks and reported all this to Dick Thompson, who in turn, unknown to me at the time, passed this praise to the head office of the Lord Chancellor's Department in the House of Lords.

I had managed to secure an unfurnished flat in Bryanston Street near Marble Arch, which I shared with my brother, John. I used to drive to the law courts from my flat in the morning in my Triumph Spitfire, hood down with a black leather jacket and sunglasses, thinking I was frightfully smooth and dashingly elegant. I must have been very irritating to any onlooker.

We had a great time there in swinging London in the early 1970s. Sometimes up to a dozen people would stay the night in my flat in Bryanston Street and in the morning we would walk over to Hyde Park to play football. We would invite Emma to be seated five yards away from Fiona. Fifty yards away Jane and Charlotte would be similarly placed. They were the goalposts! But confusion reigned when the goal posts moved closer together to chat.

I often went to the theatre including going to *Abelard and Heloise* with a seat on the left of the front row to see Diana Rigg advance nude towards me. Unfortunately, I had bought a seat on the wrong side of the theatre and so had to admire how well-endowed the formidable Australian actor Keith Michel was, as he advanced towards me!

In 1971 I joined the Hurlingham Club, a magnificent institution in sixty acres next to the Thames at Fulham. I became keen on tennis and even played for the second six before my second serve was identified as a weakness and I was dropped. I remember reciting Shakespeare, at some length on a bridge there at midnight in a white dinner jacket to an attractive girl I was attempting to woo. She was plainly, if politely, bored.

I soon realised I needed to do something worthwhile in my spare time. So I went down to HMS *President*, a floating ship on the Embankment in London, which was the headquarters of the London Division of the Royal Naval Reserve, the naval version of the Territorial Army. There was a recruiting night on a Tuesday evening so I proceeded there to be interviewed by a petty officer with a large number of World War II ribbons on his chest. I had turned up in my stiff collar looking self-important. He took one look at me and barked, 'I suppose that you want to become a f-----g officer.' I replied that no, I would join as an able seaman and if no good would stay an able seaman. He said this was the attitude he liked to hear, but I would join as an ordinary seaman, provided, of course, I could pass the naval intelligence test. So I was firmly put in my place. I passed this test and joined the Royal Naval Reserve as an ordinary seaman and went off to sea in minesweepers. I learned how to steer the ship and coil down flexible steel wire ropes; I studied the purpose and function of head ropes and springs and learned basic navigation. I particularly remember on my first trip proceeding down Southampton Water. While hauling in the large fenders on the sweep deck I remarked to the first lieutenant, a partner at Freshfields solicitors, that this was perhaps the most exciting moment in my life. He looked rather astonished at this but did recognise my enthusiasm.

At this time, Sir Denis Dobson, QC, the permanent secretary of the Lord Chancellor's Department in the House of Lords, decided he wanted to see if there was any talent among the numerous outstations of the department. The Lord Chancellor's Department included the Land Registry, the Criminal Injuries Compensation Board, the Law Commission, the Criminal Appeal Office and other small legal establishments.

Early in 1974 each boss of these organisations was asked to nominate two lawyers for further interviews. There were thirty lawyers in the Criminal Appeal Office so I did not think I stood a chance. Yet, much to my surprise, I was one of the two selected by dear Dick Thompson. I suppose the kind words of Edmund Davies had something to do with it.

The other person from my office to be selected was a lady and lawyer of distinction, Pat Edwards, who subsequently became the deputy ombudsman. I sallied forth to be interviewed in the House of Lords by a knight of the realm and two officials from the Lord Chancellor's Department. I was doing only moderately well at this interview, especially when asked, 'Hanratty, tell us about the law of forgery.' As I began to recite some of the dimly remembered provisions of the Forgery Act, the radiator blew up. It was like an Icelandic geyser or the steam from Rotorua in New Zealand. The board cowered but I assumed the role of Able Seaman Hanratty and leapt into action. I turned the radiator off, pulled down the bomb proof curtains, plugged the leak, and with studied nonchalance turned towards the board and asked, 'Now gentlemen where were we?' Fortunately they had forgotten. The rest of the interview was much more relaxed and the questions less demanding. I have no independent evidence of this but I suspect Sir Denis Dobson, the permanent secretary received a report along the lines of 'Hanratty does not know much law but is jolly good in a crisis!'

The end result was that of the thirty or so lawyers who had been selected for interview six of us went through to the second round for an interview with the great Sir Denis himself. I turned up to find, astonishingly, we were wearing exactly the same clothes: a fine pin-stripe suit with a blue shirt and a white stiff collar and very shiny Church's shoes. This was a good start, which should have been irrelevant but was not in those days.

Sir Denis was tall, silver haired, elegant and frightening. He seated me on a low chair so that my bottom was touching the ground and he could gaze down haughtily upon me from on high. I said I did not think this was very comfortable for him or for me. I insisted on sitting on a chair broadly the same height as his chair. So I, as it were, had stood up to him. I was thoroughly grilled about the law and policy and the way government worked.

Fortunately, I had carefully read the brilliant book *Anatomy of Britain* by Anthony Sampson as well as his subsequent book *Who Runs this Place?* These and a further book by Bernard Levin intimately described how government actually worked and how legislation happened with influences from professional bodies, the trade unions and political parties and their manifestos. They explained the mechanics of legislation and the competing pressures and compromises which had to be made in order for legislation to be passed. The influence of the civil servants, of public corporations, nationalised industries, trade unions, the Bank of England and pressure groups from farmers to the church and insurance bodies were all carefully described. I was fascinated by all this and was a master of this detail. This was surprising to Sir Denis and it clearly impressed him. He was also pleased by my service in the Royal Naval Reserve as by this time I had just been awarded my commission as a sub-lieutenant after a series of demanding exams both at sea and ashore.

At that time, nearly all the senior officials in the Lord Chancellor's Department had served in the war. There was a captain of a motor torpedo boat and there were intelligence officers and front line officers who had fought all the way from D-Day in Normandy to Germany. These included the intellectual Sir Wilfrid Bourne who succeeded Sir Denis. Wilfrid had landed the day after D-Day as a young nineteen-year-old junior officer in the light infantry straight out of Eton. He fought his way to Germany. He was an intellectual, a humble and brilliant man and an accomplished sailor. Sir Denis called him in and Wilfrid asked me some further questions on secondary legislation. I passed muster. Sir Denis announced that in two weeks' time I was to start work in the House of Lords as one of the fifteen legal advisors to the Lord Chancellor; not bad for a lawyer who had not been to university and who had emerged from obscurity in Derbyshire. I owed my former colleagues in the Criminal Appeal Office an enormous debt and personally visited Dick Thompson to thank him.

4

PAM

It was about this time in 1974 that I met Pam, then known as Pamela Hoare, at the Hurlingham Club, where we were both members and both keen tennis players. On one occasion we were bracketed together to play a tennis match against another club. Pam's father, a Royal Marine gunnery officer, had actually played at Wimbledon shortly after the war and got through to the second round. He was a fine tennis player. In any event, the match was cancelled. I had given up a weekend on a minesweeper to play the match so I telephoned the formidable lady who ran all the tennis courts at Hurlingham, Miss Diggins, and requested one so that four of us from our team of six could have a friendly doubles. When Pam turned up I realised within about ten minutes that she was the girl for me. I remarked, Joan Hunter Dunn style, that I admired her backhand and suggested dinner at 235 Kings Road, then the first bistro in London. Off we went.

I wooed her like mad after that. I even wrote a few love letters to her but being a lawyer they did not sound very spontaneous as they had been through a dozen drafts. I promised to treat her like a queen. Occasionally, I am reminded about this when I fail to come up to expectations. I went to see her parents in Cobham in Surrey, where I was largely ignored. Her Canadian mother barely raised her fork while tending to their pretty garden. I realised straight away that I was the latest in rather a long line of suitors.

When I took Pam up to Derbyshire to meet my own parents my formal mother escorted Pam to her room. Then she came down stairs, passed me in the hall and without looking at me and in a Lady Bracknell voice said, 'If you ever lose her I shall never forgive you.' Pam never stood a chance after that! But the great day came when I took Pam to the top of the Post Office Tower and, in the revolving restaurant, I formally proposed to her. She was very embarrassed and replied, 'Oh yes, of course, but do please pass the butter.' I still remind her of that moment to this day.

Her father was a brave and decorated gunnery officer in the Royal Marines, while her grandfather was a Captain RN who sailed around Cape Horn in a schooner during a storm before World War I. Her uncle was Rear Admiral Desmond Hoare who was the founding headmaster of Atlantic College in Wales, the first of the United World Colleges. He also patented the first Rigid-Inflatable Boat (RIB). To the chagrin of the family he sold the patent to the RNLI for a pound. Hence the inshore lifeboats are still called 'The Atlantic Class'. Pam's great grandfather, Alexander Buntin emigrated to Canada in 1837 from Scotland and was a most successful businessman, who founded a paper mill and the well-known insurance company Sun Life. His portrait hangs above our fireplace. The children call him 'Alexander the Great'.

Pam was educated at St Teresa's Convent in Dorking and at a Swiss finishing school. Here in a beautiful mountain range above Aigle she learned 'Franglais' and the art of skiing. It was very strict and the girls were warned by the headmistress that men were 'dangerous'. At the age of twenty-one she emigrated to South Africa with a friend. She found a job working for the manager of the Turf Club in Cape Town and then travelled all over the beautiful country, including to south-west Africa. When her funds began to run dry, she stayed for six months in Johannesburg and worked for a lawyer. After two years away, she made the journey back to the UK overland from Johannesburg to London in a three ton truck. She fended off robbers in Dar es Salaam, fought off malaria in the Cameroons and dug latrines all the way though Africa.

We became engaged within six weeks and had a lovely wedding in Esher on 31 May 1975 with a honeymoon in Greece. Pam's old boss and godfather, Sir Patrick Wall, MC, MP, who had been in the wartime Royal Marines with Pam's father, gave a witty speech. We had a guard of honour from the RNR.

Although I was not earning much compared to some of my friends in City-based law firms, we were quite well off. The RNR was a significant part of my life. Pam, with her service background loved the social life and always looked so elegant at service balls and dances.

Pam's father, who had been badly wounded in the war, needed warm weather so her parents bought a lovely villa in Vale do Lobo on the Algarve. We had many happy holidays there playing golf, tennis and relaxing in the sun. On one occasion we became great friends with a retired naval officer who spotted a Portuguese war-ship at anchor. So in the early evening he sent a signal by Morse code on a powerful torch. The ship replied. Later six young officers came ashore for a drink.

In due course Richard was born in 1977, Alexandra in 1981 and Susie in 1987. Pam and I had our fortieth wedding anniversary in 2015 and went to Venice, returning on the Orient Express. It was magnificent. We had a black tie dinner prepared by a leading French chef as we rode through the Brenner Pass. It was sheer magic.

Later, when we moved to Hong Kong, our lives were transformed. For the first time in my life I appreciated being well paid. Early in 1991 Pam joined a Dutch charity and had the very rewarding experience of helping the Vietnamese boat people with recreational activities such as sewing and painting. She also thrived in helping children to read as a voluntary assistant in Richard's school. She so loved supporting the children that it made her decide to embrace a teaching qualification on our return to England. In between, we enjoyed playing tennis, trekking over the mountains in the New Territories and sailing to remote islands with friends and their children where we swam and sang around barbeques on the beach. We thoroughly enjoyed the tranquillity well away from the hustle and bustle of the city. Three times a year we raced to Macau in our boat.

We have spent much of our social life at Hurlingham, where I was eventually voted on to the Committee at an AGM to join bright bankers and others in guiding this magnificent club set in sixty acres by the river at Fulham.

Pam is intelligent, tough and self-reliant, good looking and altogether a wonderful wife, on whom I have always depended. She is a fine and much loved mother to our three children. She is also a very competent and helpful crew member when we are out sailing. She is a proud associate member of The Royal Yacht Squadron.

Pam still teaches children with special needs at Fulham Preparatory School with sometimes spectacular results. One of her former pupils is now studying for his PhD. I have always been very proud of her.

5

THE ROYAL NAVAL RESERVE

I had joined the London Division of the Royal Naval Reserve in 1972 as an ordinary seaman, the equivalent of a private in the Army. This was sound practice by the RNR because it ensured that only those who had passed the relevant exams and shown some aptitude in training at sea could be promoted to the wardroom as an officer. It was no use having a socially acceptable chinless wonder of an officer who could hold his knife and fork correctly and describe his castle in Scotland at some length but who was incompetent on watch in fog in the Channel.

I found myself in the seamen's mess in the forepart of a Ton Class Minesweeper among some very tough characters indeed. They spoke a different language, using words like 'scran' for food. After a few drinks ashore there would be fights which I managed to avoid. Strawberry jam would be smeared on various undignified parts of the victim. Still, I learned to respect the practical ability of the sailors with whom I was at sea and became a kind of unofficial legal adviser to some of them.

The commitment in the London Division was broadly one or two evenings a week, two out of five weekends at sea and an annual fortnight at sea which was usually a NATO exercise or a patrol off the coast of Northern Ireland.

My first fortnight at sea on a NATO exercise was not a particularly happy one as the weather was really foul and I felt seasick some of the time. But I learned to steer the ship, was taught seamanship and gathered the basics of some navigation by being made the assistant to the navigating officer.

After about eighteen months I took my able seaman exams and passed. At about that time I was selected for officer training. I still wore the normal sailor uniform of bell bottoms and cap but on my shoulders a white marker was sewn to show all and sundry I was being trained as an officer. My performance was closely monitored.

This all nearly came to an end when we went for a run ashore in Cherbourg after an exercise in the Channel. We proceeded into a bar, still all in our naval ratings uniforms, and one of our group started a fight with a Frenchman for no reason at all. Twenty minutes later there was a shout. I peered out of the window to see about ten Frenchmen standing in the middle of the road shouting obscenities. At least two of them were brandishing knives. I thought this was the end of my brief legal career, so I turned to our natural leader, Leading Seaman 'Lofty' Barber who was six-foot-seven, strong and competent and asked him what I should do. He replied, 'You stick close to me.' I had no difficulty whatsoever in obeying this instruction!

We all sauntered off into the street to return to our ship trying to look as fierce as possible. Fortunately, the incident finished with insults from the French and silence from us. It was only when we had nearly arrived back at the ship that one of my number, another hardened leading seaman, showed me he had a broken glass in his pocket. I told him that if he had used this, I could have been convicted of affray or conspiracy to assault and would have been sent down with him to Parkhurst.

It was in the seamen's mess that I saw what was wrong with our education system in the UK. Here were some tough, intelligent and massively competent sailors who, because they had attended poor schools in the East End of London, had little or no formal qualifications and certainly no ambition. I advised some of them that they should become officers but they didn't wish to do so; they didn't want to lose their friends. Still, the RN and the RNR were, and still are, exceptionally good at spotting talent no matter who the person is or where he or she came from. These people were helped and encouraged to become officers and leaders. In the RN some of these talented people, who had had a difficult start in life, became admirals. This was a magnificent tribute to equal opportunity in the navy.

On board the ships we were engaged in NATO exercises which involved highly complex mine sweeping operations. This meant streaming sweeps between two vessels rather like fishermen trawling. We also would stream a complex piece of kit which pulsated an electric current to activate magnetic and other mines. In NATO exercises dummy mines would be laid and we would have to clear the path for the task force to enter a particular foreign port, often under the watchful gaze of a Russian trawler which never seemed to do any trawling but had an impressive series of aerials! On one occasion a Russian trawler came close to one of our minesweepers and through a megaphone wished our captain by name a happy birthday. The Russians knew everything. So the work was technical, quite tough and sometimes not all that pleasant but I made some very good friends and retained my sense of humour; on one occasion it was nearly my undoing.

As an able seaman I was on parade for the inspection of the London Division of the RNR in Temple Gardens, the glorious gardens of the Temple barristers' chambers. Here the whole division was lined up in platoons for inspection by the Admiral Commanding Reserves, Rear Admiral IGW Robertson. He was a senior naval officer who had last commanded HMS Eagle. So, all the senior officers were lined up with swords. A Royal Marine band was playing. The Admiral emerged from his car to a 'Royal Salute – Present Arms' from the 500 or so assembled members of the London Division. This whole event was watched by relatives and friends and by barristers and other staff leaning out of windows on a glorious summer's evening.

The Admiral in his speech was supposed to say something like, 'We in the Royal Navy are particularly grateful to you in the RNR for giving up your weekends to defend the realm and to give the hard worked Royal Navy a break. I particularly recognise and applaud your enthusiasm, professionalism and hard work....' This is what we normally received and what we all expected. But this admiral stood up and into speakers six-feet-high, heard as far as Piccadilly Circus, boomed, 'When I see one of Her Majesty's minesweepers steaming down the Solent with a seven degree list to port I do not want to be told, "But Sir, it has always been like that."' When I laughed loudly at this, our platoon commander looked around and gave me the most ferocious glare. I was given a formal dressing down afterwards and told that if this kind of behaviour 'persisted' I would remain in the ranks from which I would never, ever emerge.

In order to become an officer my social skills were sorely tested. On another occasion I was in the minesweeper, HMS *Thames*, when we visited St Malo for a formal visit. A cocktail party was arranged. The guests included the mayor, the local police chief, a few politicians and the army general of France Land Forces, West. Our captain was Henry Roberts, who was widely adored as a leader and captain. It helped that he looked like Gregory Peck.

As an able seaman upper yardman, I was deputed to greet the guests at the gangway, escort them to the wardroom, the officers' mess, and introduce them to the captain; not a particularly demanding task one would think. The first three or four guests were greeted by me and escorted without problem. Then I noticed a man with a Maigret type cap on, followed by a diminutive, waspish little French woman, coming up the gangway. So I greeted him with a 'Bienvenu' and took them both to the captain and said in my best school boy French, 'Monsieur le Capitaine je present monsieur l'Inspecteur de Police.' The little woman behind then began to shout hysterically in front of all the guests. She eventually was heard to say, 'Non, non, c'est le general.' So here was I trying to impress the captain with my social skills but I had just introduced the French general to the captain as the local copper. I stood there transfixed with my mouth wide open, utterly speechless. Henry, of course, saw the amusing side of this and gave me a wink and muttered, 'James, piss off.' Off I swiftly pissed! Fortunately this did not hold up my commission.

The great weekend then dawned in 1974 when I had to take my officer tests in Portsmouth. These included certain practical tasks at which I was not very proficient, relying on the other candidates to mutter to me what actually should be done in swinging people across imaginary chasms. Then the dreaded moment came when I was to be interviewed. I was marched in and seated in front of a Royal Navy captain and two RNR commanders, all looking rather unfriendly and fierce. After a discussion about my naval career so far, the captain gave me a car aerial. I was told to point to a large map of Europe on the wall and demonstrate where the weakest area of NATO was. Without hesitation, I pointed my aerial at Cyprus. I opined that this was the weakest link, because Greece and Turkey, both members of NATO, might well fight each other and let the Russians pour through the gap in the NATO forces.

At this point one of the wing men, an RNR Commander, went very red, even puce, and started to perspire. He then shouted at me that I was talking absolute rubbish because he had a villa in Cyprus. He blurted that the Greeks and the Turks got on frightfully well. The captain in the middle asked me whether I wished to change my mind. I told him I would stick to my guns, as it were, and I hoped the Greeks and Turks would keep theirs in their holsters too. After that I had little confidence my interview had been successful. But I heard a week later that I had been granted my commission with surprisingly high marks. Of course, as is well known, six months after this interview Turkey invaded Cyprus and took the northern part. The Greeks were left with the south. If I had been denied my commission I had my appeal papers easily ready to be drafted!

I then found myself as a sub-lieutenant RNR with one gold ring on the sleeve of my Gieves and Hawkes tailored uniform, a very proud young officer I was too. The first thing I did was join an inshore minesweeper in Dartmouth for a three week navigational cruise all the way past the Isle of Man to the north of Scotland and the Orkneys and then down to Edinburgh. This navigational cruise was a wonderful opportunity to sharpen my navigational skills. We sailed in to Douglas in the Isle of Man with an officer in a kilt on the bridge roof playing the bagpipes as we came alongside. This proved to be a great draw and many nurses, some of whom were rather wild, came on board for the cocktail party. It was a great success.

At that time I served in minesweepers in NATO exercises and in Northern Ireland patrols at the height of the Troubles. We went to Moscow Camp in Belfast to be given a lecture by some sergeant major who treated us all with contempt. He introduced his talk by announcing, 'Gentlemen, you can wipe those silly grins off your faces because you are now in a war zone.' He then proceeded to show us knee-caps, one as a consequence of an IRA bullet and the second by a so-called loyalist electric drill. That soon kept us quiet. However, I was concerned at the aggressive manner in which we were told that we were in a war zone when the mind-set should have been, in my view, that of peace-keeping. Various long-haired soldiers came on board to help us with our tasks. I realised very soon that the more dishevelled they looked, the more expert they were as Special Forces.

I was appointed 'Sub of the Gunroom' in 1977, the senior junior officer in the London Division. For my annual dinner the guest was Admiral Sir David Williams, the Second Sea Lord, an impressive and kindly man. We kept in touch afterwards. My father attended this dinner wearing his medals and told me how proud he was. Brother John, a fine Fastnet sailor, also became a sub-lieutenant. My brother Patrick joined the RNR but left after a few months as he was transferred abroad.

I passed my navigation exams with the Royal Navy, which involved a week ashore then a week at sea. We had to pass a rules-of-the-road style exam to demonstrate knowledge of international collision regulations, including sound and light signals. That exam consisted of fifty questions at two marks each. The pass mark was ninety per cent. I was doing well at this formal exam when the last question came up: 'You are entering a foreign port for the first time and see a quick flashing white light under a fixed red light. What is it?' I had worked really hard for this exam but didn't know the answer so I guessed. I was wrong. The correct answer turned out to be, 'The revolving door of a brothel.' I was furious as I told the examining officer that he had stopped me for the first time ever from getting 100 per cent in an exam. He replied that this was a lesson as 'You bastards should not think you know it all.' I conceded he had a point.

Eventually, I received my bridge watch-keeping ticket after doing the prescribed hours on watch. An experienced captain and brilliant ship handler, George Lines, told me in Calais that I would be awarded my ticket if I took the minesweeper across the Channel, up the Thames and into the Medway without too many alarms. Notwithstanding that the visibility closed in and a ship was passing the wrong way down the shipping lane, all was well. So George gave me my bridge watch-keeping ticket allowing me to run a watch even on my own.

This meant that on operations I would be in charge of the bridge as officer of the watch and usually had a more junior officer in support. It was at this time I learned a lesson for life. In a NATO exercise off Portugal our task was to sweep lanes leading into the coast. The exercise mines were laid and the lanes were marked by floating buoys with quick flashing white lights on the top of them so we could see the line ahead. When the ship reached the end of the line, she was turned and went down to sweep another lap, rather like mowing a lawn.

I came on watch one morning at 3.50 a.m., ten minutes early, to take over at 4 a.m. There were two ex-Royal Navy lieutenants on watch who gave me a short briefing. They advised that all I had to do was keep on this easterly course. The next quick flashing light was approximately at one o'clock in direction. When I reached that light I was to turn round and come back. 'Do you have the ship?' they asked. I formally said that I did and off they went.

But something worried me. There were no shore markings. It was all pitch black. There were no other ships around. No lights shone apart from this quick flashing light at about the direction of one o'clock. I went straight to the radar and put a fix on the chart using three radar ranges to the nearest points of land. My next horrified action was to call down the speaking tube to the captain in his cabin. Without waiting for him, I gave the order 'port fifteen' to turn round. The captain then came to the bridge, not too pleased to be called on a calm night, to hear my report that we were 400 yards from the beach at a speed of eight knots and a mile beyond the end of the lap.

It transpired that the signal pointed out to me was probably a white light in a house with a tree in front and the leaves waving to give the misleading impression of a quick flashing light. This light was about a mile and a half inland. I was just about to drive the minesweeper up the beach in Portugal where the revolution had recently taken place! We would not have been welcome; there would have been a major international incident. I certainly would not be writing these memoirs if I had driven that warship up a foreign beach with inevitable casualties.

Immediately there was an enquiry that found these two lieutenants had been chatting away to each other without putting regular fixes on the chart, as required. They had been relying on moving along the line of quick flashing buoys. As a reward, I was relieved of the task of doing night duties for a while and received the grateful thanks of the rest of the wardroom. The captain of the London Division, George Beatty, an experienced marine barrister, soon had these two gentlemen in front of him for an interview, without coffee. They wisely accepted the invitation to resign forthwith. George Beatty thanked me over a whisky in his cabin on board HMS *President*. I was so relieved that there had not been a disaster.

This was a lesson for life. Whenever I was succeeding someone in a job or a significant task at sea or on land I always asked for a full brief and then carefully checked it before making decisions based on that brief. If the brief was unreliable, then my decisions could be decisions built on sand. There was no doubt that if anything had gone wrong, I would have been the person to take the chop. In all my career after that, particularly in the law and in running law courts or in negotiating treaties with other countries, I always checked my brief and never really fully relied on the information that I had been given without discreet checking. The RNR had given me a warning and a lesson which I have never, ever forgotten.

I had another experience where my own reactions surprised me. On one exercise we were returning from Copenhagen across the North Sea when winds of over fifty knots, gusting sixty hit us without warning. I was on the bridge and saw this enormous vertical wall of grey water coming straight at us, rather like in the film *The Perfect Storm*. We slowly struggled on and on and upwards and then crashed down the other side. I was fascinated by my own reaction, which I carefully observed. I was not afraid at all because I knew there was nothing I could do except perform my duty in a quiet fashion like all my colleagues around me. It was not bravery, just good training, a desire not to let myself down in front of my friends and an acceptance of fate.

Eventually, I was promoted to lieutenant commander. When I went to work in the Attorney General's Chambers in Hong Kong some years later I joined the RNR unit based at HMS *Tamar*. Although I did some sea training in the patrol craft out there, the main function was with an organisation known as Naval Control of Shipping which helped brief and prepare merchant ships in the event of a war, so they could organise themselves into convoys if necessary. This included flying in a helicopter out in the South China Sea and being lowered on a wire on to the top of containers to brief masters of merchant shipping at sea. On one occasion, in my white tropical uniform and carrying a brief case, I was lowered on to the containers of a large American vessel. The Filipino crew saw this figure descending from the sky and assumed I was a customs officer intent on a surprise inspection. They instantly vanished. I was stranded three containers up before a ladder was eventually secured for me to descend. I received the Reserve Decoration (RD) in 1987 for, as I suspected, fifteen years of undetected crime in the RNR!

On one occasion in Hong Kong I was invited on board a US warship to be shown round by a very bright young American lieutenant. I was accompanied in uniform by my great friend Clive, also a lieutenant commander. We were joined by an American full commander, a swarthy Italian American with a name like Capello in large letters on his left breast. We were shown round this warship and the young American officer pointed to the gun on the bow and asked me whether I was familiar with it. I replied that it was an Italian gun with a range of about twelve thousand yards; it was the same as was on the Peacock class of patrol craft used then in Hong Kong by the Royal Navy. He said that was absolutely right and, before he could carry on, my friend Clive blurted, 'James what happens when an Italian fires a gun?' I said that I did not know. He replied, 'It goes pop and out comes a white flag.' Then we looked up and saw the swarthy Italian American commander, who out ranked him, standing there fuming with rage.

Ever quick on his feet, Clive stood to attention and proclaimed, 'Sir, I regret that remark. It was never made. I never, ever meant it if it was made. I have full respect for Italians and the American Navy. I apologise, Sir.' The American officer nodded and said nothing.

In response, all I managed to do was crawl round the other side of this gun turret on the deck of this American warship to try to hide the fact that I wanted to howl with prolonged laughter. I can say categorically to any doctor that the symptoms of a person who wishes to howl with laughter but is prevented from doing so are a pain down the side of the ribs and tears flooding down one's cheeks. These are precisely the symptoms I had when I heard the apology from Clive and saw the reaction of this poor, unfortunate but clearly wronged American Italian officer. I have dined out on this story for years.

Eventually, in about 1994, I was asked by the admiralty whether I would be returning to England from Hong Kong; they were offering me the prospect of promotion to commander. I replied I could not do so until 1997, after the handover of Hong Kong to China was complete. So, after twenty-two years in the RNR, I retired with a delightful and generous three page letter from the admiralty to thank me for what I had done. I remain in contact with many of my former colleagues in the RNR through the President Retired Officers Association from HMS *President*, the headquarters of the London Division of the RNR, and also through Hong Kong friends and the RNVR Yacht Club.

6
LORD CHANCELLOR'S DEPARTMENT
1974 – 1981

My first day at the Lord Chancellor's Department in the House of Lords was spent in various security checks. I presume there were raised eyebrows concerning how I had managed to arrive there. Eventually, I was shown to my desk in what was universally known as 'the nursery'. This was a large office on the ground floor of the Royal Court where junior lawyers traditionally first sat. I shared this room with two other lawyers, one a former naval lawyer, Peter Harris, who subsequently became Official Solicitor and had a fine reputation for defending the needs of children. The other was an intellectual Old Etonian, Michael Collon, who subsequently became the secretary of the Law Commission. Both were charming, friendly and able. There was a tradition then, owing to official secrets, that when the last person left the room the door was locked. That first day they obviously forgot about my quiet presence in the corner because at lunchtime they both got up and instinctively locked me in. Early on I learned the vital importance of never having the waste paper basket next to the desk lest some secret papers landed in it to be carted off to a skip in Wandsworth.

My first task in the Lord Chancellor's Department was to represent the Lord Chancellor on negotiations in Whitehall on possible implementation of the European Bankruptcy Convention. I knew nothing about bankruptcy apart from a desire to try to avoid it. But I burned the midnight oil reading a particularly impressive paper from Professor Anton from Scotland that argued the European Bankruptcy Convention was utterly incompatible with the practice of our own bankruptcy law and we would not be able to join it. On day two I was despatched to a meeting at the Department of Trade with representatives from the Insolvency

Service and senior practitioners. Having been up half the night studying, I tried to give an impression, which I am sure convinced no one, of some knowledge of the subject. I mentioned the salient points from the paper and, to my surprise, found favour. Eventually, it was agreed that the European Bankruptcy Convention could not become part of our law. This was my first introduction into European law. It was to become useful in the later part of my career in international law, particularly as an immigration judge.

At that time Lord Elwyn-Jones was the Welsh Labour Lord Chancellor. He was a man of great charm and wit. I was asked to see him on one occasion to explain a particular clause in an Administration of Justice Bill which I had been negotiating and working on with a parliamentary draftsman. When I saw him he smiled and asked, 'Now James is this a good socialist measure?' I replied, 'Lord Chancellor I am singularly ill qualified to answer that question but the measure would be popular, cheap and easy to administer.' Lord Elwyn-Jones replied, 'In that case James it is a good socialist measure. You may go and proceed.'

He was very fond of Welsh jokes in his after-dinner speeches including one of my favourites. Three MPs were driving on a Welsh hillside and were hopelessly lost in the mist. They then saw a shepherd with his flock on the side of the road. So they stopped the car, wound down the window and asked, 'Could you please help us. Where are we?' The shepherd replied, 'In a car.' One of the MPs remarked, 'that is the perfect answer to a parliamentary question, it is short; it is true; and does not give away any more information than was otherwise previously available.'

On one occasion I got into minor trouble as I was the advisor on an uncontentious bill going through the House of Commons. We were stuck in Committee because the opposition Tories had asked numerous questions on the bill which delayed matters and were not helpful. I found myself in the stand-ups in a House of Commons loo peeing next to Ian Percival, then the Tory shadow Solicitor-General. I turned to him, fortunately without wetting his shiny shoes, and asked, 'Mr Percival why are you delaying this bill? You really must know it would be a very useful and uncontentious measure which is not politically divisive.' He looked at me and said, 'My dear boy, you really will have to learn the subtleties of House of Commons life. I suggest you don't do that again.'

He then had a quiet word with the private secretary to the Lord Chancellor. I was not given a reprimand, just a quiet piece of advice. I was right in that the bill would have been useful and was not politically divisive. But it turned out I was entirely wrong to have tackled Ian Percival about it. The Tories were deliberately delaying this bill in committee to prevent another one which was, indeed, politically divisive, from reaching the committee stage. So the bill I was involved in was a barrier to prevent the storms of another bill flooding the committee with controversy at a later date. Moreover, as an official, I should never have spoken to a shadow minister like that.

One of my tasks during my time at the Lord Chancellor's Department was to steer part of another Administration of Justice Bill with a bankruptcy element to it through Parliament. One day we were in the House of Commons on the second reading when halfway through the so-called 'Beast of Bolsover', Dennis Skinner, MP, got up and laid in, 'My brother who is a Clay Cross councillor has been removed from office and made bankrupt with other councillors in a politically motivated attack on freedom of speech. What do you say about that?' This was not in the brief. The minister looked towards me and I shrugged my shoulders as if you say, 'You're on your own mate.'

In fact, I vaguely knew Dennis Skinner, an MP of integrity. His brother was a patient of my father. One day my father was about to go to a wedding wearing a morning coat and was called out to see Dennis Skinner's brother. He turned up to find Dennis there too. My father explained his formal attire by saying it was only right that when he visited the brother of an MP with the MP present he should dress up for the occasion. He was never sure whether his remark was recognised as the joke that it was.

In any event, the bill was passed. My superior, Roland Widdows, who had driven an MTB during the war remarked that my 'Notes on Clauses' were the best that he had ever seen. I rather spoiled the praise by saying that I had just been on the course!

In those days there were only about fifteen lawyers working closely with the Lord Chancellor. The senior officials were all lawyers who gave themselves legal advice and carried out managerial functions. This was the only department which had this rather odd arrangement. In most other departments the lawyers were a separate entity who would occasionally be consulted and were not always treated with the respect they deserved. Foreign Office lawyers, for example, were known as 'reptiles' by the diplomats.

By today's standards the appointments process was far from politically correct. Nearly all the lawyers came from top public schools like Rugby, Eton and Winchester and had high quality degrees from Oxbridge. They were very hard-working and devoted, knowing, as I did, there were hundreds of lawyers behind them who would give their right arm to have the same opportunity. Indeed, Sir Denis Dobson used to walk around the office at about 8 p.m. to make sure we were still at our desks. If any lawyer was not up to standard, out they would go the next afternoon. There were no ethnic minorities among the senior staff and very few women. The only women, in fact, who were in posts tended to be the daughters of High Court judges. Yet, in spite of the lack of managerial experience, the Lord Chancellor would receive the most detailed, thoughtful and sound advice from extremely able lawyers, with a deep knowledge of Whitehall.

Much to my relief, I was eventually moved away from bankruptcy and put in charge of the legal aid arrangements. I became secretary of a body called the Legal Aid Legislation Working Party consisting of officials and members of the judiciary. The Lord Chancellor was keen that there should not be an unmet need for legal services and wanted those who brought cases before the courts to have the benefit of legal aid where the merits and financial tests were satisfied. There was also a growth in Law Centres around the country, some funded by local authorities but others out of central funds. Richard White was brought down from Birmingham University to demonstrate the unmet need for legal services in a wide ranging report. I like to think that the legal aid system worked well and that those who were deserving of financial support in court cases received it. I became something of an expert on legal aid.

Eventually, I was promoted and was allowed to take my turn in attending meetings of the management board of the department consisting of the permanent secretary, two deputy secretaries and various undersecretaries. I was not supposed to contribute, merely to sit in the corner and listen and learn.

Another duty, which occasionally arose, was that on Saturday mornings we, more junior lawyers, took it in turn to sit in the desk of the private secretary to the Lord Chancellor to handle any emergencies or difficulties.

One Saturday I was doing this and to my surprise Sir Denis himself turned up. He was Clerk of the Crown in Chancery, an ancient office, which had a function that involved checking by-election results. There had been a by-election the day before. He came into the private office to find me sitting there, trying to look as though I knew what was going on, and asked me to get the telephone number of an official. I had to explain that this official had gone to Scotland on holiday and was in some croft entirely out of contact. He then looked at the notice board behind me and saw that another official who had retired ten years earlier still had his telephone number displayed. He barked at me, 'What is Thesiger's telephone number doing there?' I said I did not know but perhaps he was still being used as a consultant and, in any event, only the private secretary, John Watherston, himself would know.

Sir Denis decided he would therefore tackle me. He said, 'When you go to sea in your bloody minesweeper do you use charts ten years old?' I replied, 'Sir Denis it is a happy coincidence that you should ask that because I have just been on a navigational cruise in the Western Isles of Scotland and could not help noticing that the charts were drafted by a Captain Hydrographer Royal Navy in, (pause), 1856!' Sir Denis stopped in his tracks, looked at me and I am sure he winked. He quietly shut the door into his own office and the whole of the rest of my time with him in the Lord Chancellor's Department was entirely trouble free. It was a classic example of standing up to a person who was trying to catch me out, having a go, even slightly bullying. Nevertheless, I always had enormous respect for him.

At that time I used to cycle to the House of Lords from where Pam and I lived in Putney. One day I was knocked off my bicycle by a Mercedes turning right from the opposite direction on the Embankment. I went right over the top of the bonnet. My helmet smashed into it and I landed on the road the other side. The smooth driver got out, did not bother to ask how I was but opined I had caused £800 worth of damage to his car. From a sitting position on the road I replied he may have caused £250,000 of damage because I was unsure whether I could ever walk again. He drove off leaving me with a mangled bike. I shuffled to a door in Tite Street and knocked.

Much to my surprise a beautiful Vision of a goddess appeared in a dressing gown made entirely of feathers. I apologised and asked whether I could use her phone. She took me to her bedroom where, in the middle of a huge heart shaped bed, was a phone. I crawled towards it followed by the Vision. I had to explain to her that, notwithstanding my fit and lean appearance, I would not be able to oblige her as, firstly, I was hurt and, secondly, I was asking my wife to come to the rescue! The kind Vision went off to make me a cup of tea. Pam eventually arrived to drive me and the bike to Westminster. The Vision subsequently received a huge bunch of flowers delivered, not by me, but by Interflora. I think she may have been 'on the game' but had a heart of gold. Three hours later I began to tremble with delayed shock. I was taken to Westminster

Hospital. The A&E doctor said my helmet had saved my life and I should warn other cyclists to wear one.

Meanwhile, Pam, Richard and I moved into a slightly larger house in Putney in time for Alexandra to be born in January 1981. It was around that time, I noticed in *The Times* an advertisement for lawyers in the Attorney General's Chambers in Hong Kong. I learned that these chambers were very similar to the Lord Chancellor's Department. The new Attorney General, John Griffiths, QC, a renowned English silk, was trying to raise the standard of the place and was looking for new lawyers to fly out from England. There were 400 applications for sixteen places. I was interviewed and I think, largely because I was in the Lord Chancellor's Department rather than any personal qualities that I may have had, I was offered a relatively senior position.

Pam and I then had a major dilemma over whether or not to go. I feared I might never be able to return to the department, or that I might find subordinates promoted in my absence. Pam had just given birth to Alexandra and was too tired to travel. Over long walks on Wimbledon Common we decided to go, largely on the basis that I did not want to spend the rest of my life regretting an opportunity lost. I did not want to be a frustrated civil servant holding on to his greasy lunchtime sandwiches while grimly shuffling over Westminster Bridge in a blue mac to work, wondering for the rest of his life what might have been.

Once I had made my decision I had to go to the permanent secretary to ask whether I could be released on leave of absence. I would be away for three or four years but then would have the right of return. To my relief the permanent secretary, by this time Sir Derek Oulton, QC, felt that this would be a good opportunity for me to acquire wider experience. He most generously allowed me to take leave of absence. I had a farewell party and then I was off.

Still, it was a huge upheaval. I had to leave Pam and the children behind. She had to pack up the house, deal with agents and inventories and correspondence of many kinds and then let the house. As ever, she coped well. The plane was over Austria before I stopped crying. I would not see her or the children for three months.

7

HONG KONG 1981 – 1985

As Alexandra had only just been born it would have been unfair on Pam and the children to travel to Hong Kong at the beginning of my contract. So I flew in advance, in early February 1981. I found myself staying in the Lee Gardens Hotel in Causeway Bay until a flat was available for me and the family. It was a large four star hotel of many storeys which has since been pulled down. When I eventually left, I was asked in a survey about my experience of the three months I had stayed there. I replied that I was extremely sorry to be leaving my room, although it tended to be moist and cold from the air conditioning, because it meant saying goodbye to Walter, the cockroach. Each morning when I was shaving in front of the mirror Walter would emerge from the sink.

While I was shaving we would converse at some length about the legislation I was drafting. As he had no firm views on the matter, he would disappear again. I got very fond of my pet cockroach. I mentioned all this in the survey. Then I received a reply from a totally humourless Chinese manager who wrote in uncertain English that he was grateful for my comments. He told me that Walter would be exterminated. I replied that I was truly heart-broken, but never had a further reply from him.

In the Attorney General's Chambers I started by undertaking law drafting, both primary and secondary legislation. Many of the draftsmen were lawyers from Australia, New Zealand, Ireland and also Goa. Indeed, the lawyer from Goa, Gerry Nazareth, was so brilliant that he eventually became a judge in the highest court in Hong Kong. When the law had been drafted the lawyer appeared before the Executive Council of Hong Kong, broadly the cabinet. It was presided over by the governor, Sir Murray MacLehose, a fluent Chinese speaker, and a former mandarin in the Foreign and Commonwealth Office, who seemed to own half of Scotland. He did not take prisoners.

One day I appeared before the Executive Council, a body somewhat similar to the cabinet, as I had been drafting some financial provisions. I had taken the opportunity to tidy up the legislation by removing the word 'dollars' and inserting the symbol for dollars. A leading Chinese businessman on the Executive Council asked me what the purpose of this was. It was a quiet morning so I decided the time had come for a bit of fun. I started to explain to him that there really was no difference between the word 'dollar' and the symbol for dollar. They were, actually, of equal value. I was just beginning to enjoy myself when I looked up to see an extremely red-faced governor in front of me, shaking his head. He was less than amused and quite rightly so. I desisted abruptly by saying I was merely making the legislation consistent in order to be helpful.

The role included going before the Legislative Council, broadly Parliament in Hong Kong, to deliver a speech and answer questions from the councillors about the legislation. This was different from the UK where the official was stuck in the box in the House of Commons but did not speak. Here, not only did I speak but I also had to answer questions. There is nothing like the feeling of knowing you will be asked numerous questions about a certain legislation, possibly on TV, to cause the burning of midnight oil.

I also took time out to do some prosecuting in the district courts where the proceedings were conducted in English but with a Cantonese interpreter as the accused was usually a local Chinese citizen who did not speak English. This experience was very helpful years later when I became an immigration judge and learned how to deal with interpreters; they are invisible and must interpret precisely what is said without giving evidence.

At that time there was a fixation with homosexuality in official circles; to be gay and practising was actually a criminal offence, even for an adult. Eventually, a Royal Hong Kong policeman, a British citizen, was revealed as having a Chinese boyfriend and was found dead, shot five times. There was a rigorous enquiry. On the facts it seemed he had been murdered but forensic evidence showed an automatic weapon fired by his own hand could release five shots. Nevertheless, there was talk of a cover up in the corridors of power. The politics of it all became very unpleasant. Fortunately, I was not involved in the handling of this unpleasant business.

Pam, Richard and Alexandra arrived after three months to join me in a high-rise flat on the twenty-fourth floor with spectacular views overlooking the East Lamma Channel where all the ships would pass on their way to Hong Kong Harbour, including the *QE2*. It was spacious and we grew pretty pink bougainvillea with thorny branches to prevent the children from climbing over the balcony. We found a wonderful Filipina maid called Cirila who had her own quarters attached to the flat. Richard started at a nursery school in our block of flats and eventually attended Kellett School. Both children were happy.

In 1983 we found ourselves in the middle of Typhoon Ellen. Around 50,000 Hong Kong people were made homeless, twenty-six ships ran aground in Hong Kong harbour, some right in front of our flat. The winds reached over 100 mph. We had to keep clear of the balcony glass doors as they were bulging in the wind. Water seeped into the dining room under the wooden floorboards fully fifteen feet from the glass doors. In another flat the glass doors did smash and a piano was sucked out from twenty floors up to be shattered into many pieces below. Fortunately, only eight were killed as the people of Hong Kong were disciplined to stay in and not to move. There were landslides all over the place. The silence after the storm was eerie.

Later in that year I travelled to China, which had just opened its doors after the Cultural Revolution. I went first; Pam went later. My initial impressions were of grey pollution and millions of cyclists riding slowly and unsmilingly in a trance. The women did not wear makeup and wore drab clothing. The Chinese were still suspicious of foreigners. I climbed the magnificent Great Wall and visited the Terracotta Army in Sian where there was row upon row of fascinating soldier statues representing the armies of Qin Shi Huang, the first emperor of China. They had been recently unearthed and were buried near to the royal tomb to protect him in his afterlife. In Shanghai I had a very political guide. He declared that, 'Before liberation in 1949 there were 30,000 prostitutes. Now there are none.' The amusing Germans at the back of the bus told him that, therefore, they wanted to go home!

That evening I went for a walk on The Bund. A man approached me and whispered to me in traditional cloak and dagger fashion whether I would like a girl. He interpreted my refusal as one of sexual inclination rather than morality so he asked me whether I wanted a little boy. I invited him to clear off with some choice words, which he clearly understood. The next day on the bus the guide asked us how we had enjoyed Shanghai. It was too good an opportunity to miss. So I said, 'Do you remember how you said yesterday that before liberation there were 30,000 prostitutes in Shanghai and now there are none? Well, from my own personal experience last night, there are still at least two and only one of them is a woman.' It brought the house down. But I was a marked man for the rest of the trip after that – and I deserved it.

Many of us found learning Cantonese very difficult. One day I visited a dentist from Birmingham. He was listening to a radio programme *Barefoot Cantonese*. The woman said something in Cantonese and then translated it as 'Have you got a bigger one?' With a wild drill in my mouth the dentist roared with laughter. I did not go there again.

In 1983 the Commonwealth Law Conference took place in Hong Kong. This consisted of 3,000 delegates from all over the Commonwealth including judges, politicians and others concerned with the law or administration of justice. A large programme of social events, where no expense was spared, was organised. This was showcase time for Hong Kong. Lord Chancellor Hailsham was due to fly out to open this conference but the arrangements for his programme were a shambles and his private office in London did not know what was going on. The permanent secretary then contacted me quietly and asked me if I could possibly take charge of the schedule for the Lord Chancellor.

So I released myself from other duties and concentrated on fixing a detailed programme for the Lord Chancellor, his daughter Mary, who subsequently became a High Court judge in England, and the permanent secretary, Sir Derek Oulton himself. I had a flow chart showing what time events happened and who would be doing what and where and how they got there. I began to receive correspondence from London expressing relief that someone actually had a grip on proceedings.

One issue was where the Lord Chancellor would sleep. He was not capable of walking up the large circular stairway in Government House and there was no lift. I tried to get a sedan chair organised so he could be carried up to the bedroom in some style but, unfortunately, at a rehearsal, we were unable to get the ends of the sedan chair around the corners of the spiral staircase. So, a special bedroom was arranged for him on the ground floor. All of this emphasised the importance of 'walking the course'.

This was particularly clear when I asked to see the Convention Centre where the Lord Chancellor was due to make the opening speech in front of 3,000 delegates. There was a dais, a lectern and steps up to the dais with risings of about eighteen inches alongside a single rail. I told the organisers that if these arrangements were in place tomorrow there would be no speech from the Lord Chancellor because he would not be able to climb on to the dais to deliver his speech. But, I said, as this was Hong Kong, it should be no problem to make new steps overnight. They were made with rails on both sides and risings of no more than six inches.

We then went out to the Convention Centre for the opening ceremony. I was in the car with the Lord Chancellor and had helped him previously with his speech, not that he needed it. Lord Hailsham gave a magnificent speech about the common law, touching on the way it developed, protected the innocent, helped commerce and was a reliable indicator of the prosperity and freedom in a state. There were plenty of classical allusions. It was masterful and beautifully delivered. At the end of it he asked me how it had gone and I replied in typical courtier-like fashion, 'Lord Chancellor, you are the finest Roman of them all.' From that moment onwards he treated me like a favourite grandson. I greatly revered him.

That night there was a magnificent ball at the Regent Hotel in Kowloon. Pam looked radiant in her new pearls and a spectacular Diane Freis dress as we danced the night away, overlooking the Hong Kong Harbour at night, one of the world's most spectacular sights.

One lunchtime there was nothing officially planned so I arranged a private lunch in the Regent Hotel with Lord Chancellor Hailsham. I remarked that, as he had been First Lord of the Admiralty in 1956 and his mother was American, how would he like to apply both these connections by flying out to an American aircraft carrier, the USS *Carl Vinson*, on Saturday afternoon. He replied, 'Oh Hanratty, if you can arrange it that would be marvellous.' Of course I had already done so.

We flew out in a Scout helicopter and landed on the flight deck of the enormous American aircraft carrier to be greeted by Vice Admiral Brown. We were shown around some of the main features where the Lord Chancellor could walk. We were entertained to light eats. Then the Lord Chancellor was presented with a spectacular framed photograph of the ship from the air inscribed, 'To the Lord High Chancellor of Great Britain from Vice Admiral Brown' with the date. I was really impressed because I knew the Americans had had only about three days warning. They were very hospitable and highly professional. At the end of his time in Hong Kong, the

Lord Chancellor himself gave me a photograph of an oil painting of himself with a kind personal note written on it which is framed and happily hangs on the wall in my home to this day.

During our time out there we had some exotic and spectacular holidays, including trips to Australia and New Zealand, Sri Lanka, the Seychelles and South Africa and lastly to Hawaii and North America. We drove up from San Francisco all the way to Vancouver and through the Rockies to Calgary, where we flew to join some of Pam's Canadian relatives in Ottawa. From there we took a Greyhound bus to Montreal and then down to Boston.

When we visited the Franz Joseph Glacier in New Zealand, the amusing muscle bound Maori guide pointed to a snow cave thirty-feet deep caused by the grinding ice over centuries and observed that, 'I was brought up in that snow hole for the first twenty years of my life before I became civilised.' The blue-rinsed American female tourists exclaimed in awe, 'Oh really!' I told him quietly that he had just doubled his tip.

We travelled all around New Zealand in a campervan for four weeks. While we were in Wellington I called upon the senior legislative counsel, the equivalent of the first parliamentary counsel in London, because I had met him at the Commonwealth Law Conference. He looked slightly astonished at my Nike running shoes but I was wearing my only tropical suit. He complained, with some justification, about the casual hospitality he had received in London on a formal visit to his opposite numbers when he had been given a light and hasty lunch in the House of Commons canteen. I felt ashamed. He showed me round the Parliament building which was built by Sir Basil Spence to resist earthquakes of nine on the Richter scale. We then enjoyed two weeks in Australia. We travelled from Sydney to Canberra and Melbourne.

On another trip, as we drove from Vancouver to Calgary through the Rockies, we hired a recorder with a tape that acted as a guide. I drove while Pam operated the kit. She switched it on and a voice said, 'Hello, my name is Jim. Please travel at fifty-five miles per hour and switch me on again in three minutes…' This went on for about half an hour. Eventually, Jim said, 'If you look out of your right hand window you will see Mount Edith Cavell, named after a First World War heroine who was a brave nurse, shot by the Germans.'

We looked out of the window and there was no mountain there at all. It was as flat as the Lincolnshire countryside. There followed an almighty row as I told Pam she had not been keeping a proper eye on the clock. She accused me of going too fast. A simple solution would have been to motor on for another five or ten miles, take a fix, find out where we were and continue. But that was not what I did. In classic Basil Fawlty behaviour, I slammed on the brakes, did a U-turn, drove thirty miles back to the start and shouted, 'Right, we start again!' This was, of course, not an effective use of time, nor did it do anything for the relationship between me and my wife. Years later, when I was asked to give a speech on management and time management at the Civil Service College in Sunningdale, I recalled this story as an example of precisely how not to behave. Nevertheless, the Rockies were spectacular and vast.

While living in Hong Kong I had also taken the opportunity to become really athletically fit. I became so obsessed with running I was even elected to the committee of the Hong Kong Distance Runners Club, where I met Jane Plumptre, a prosecutor, who also became an immigration judge, and in 1983 ran the London Marathon in a time of 3 hours 14 minutes. The family turned out to cheer me home.

Apart from cricket, tennis and running I also became part of the Attorney General's Chambers dragon boat team for the Dragon Boat Festival. These long craft with about forty paddlers in them were directed by a barrister from Chambers banging an enormous drum on the stern in order for us to keep time, rather like the slaves in old Roman galleys. On the day of the races down at Stanley in the south of Hong Kong it was very hot and there was a fairly strong wind which meant the sea had higher waves than usual. We started our race against a Chinese fishermen's team, far better and more practised than us and an Australian and a French team.

Our drummer, a well-known lawyer and prosecutor, became increasingly overexcited by this event and began to drum faster and faster as though he was about to have an orgasm. The consequence was that we were not able to keep up and splashed water inside the boat from the disturbed sea. Suddenly, the boat stopped and we realised we were sinking. The boat slowly submerged but fortunately floated about a foot under the water enabling us all to hold on in the warm sea. After what seemed an age, a rescue boat arrived and towed the boat to the shore with us clinging on. In a bedraggled and depressed state, to raucous cheers from hundreds of other competitors and families, we trudged ashore well and truly in last place.

And so it was, in a somewhat downhearted state of mind in 1985, I was warned by the permanent secretary of the Lord Chancellor's Department that, unless I returned to the UK at the end of my agreed four years period of absence I would not be allowed back; the agreement had been that I had four years leave of absence from the department. After that it was either to stay in Hong Kong and sever all links with the department or return to the fray in London. I had to make up my mind. It was not an easy decision to make. The many benefits of living in Hong Kong were considerable compared to returning to a gloomy United Kingdom. But after much consideration, we decided reluctantly to leave; after all, England was our home.

So we said goodbye to Cirila, our Filipina maid. As a reward for her loyalty we undertook to pay the school fees of her niece in the Philippines, who without those fees would have had to leave school at the age of twelve. We eventually paid for her all the way through high school and for a computer studies course at a university. We never ever met her but we would receive her school reports and lovely cards from her at Christmas, Easter and on our birthdays. We still get these cards. It was a very heart-warming gesture that we made; and we found it actually rewarded us. It was heartily deserved by Cirila, who eventually went off to Vancouver in Canada.

I was 'mugged' in the Attorney General's Chambers, the traditional farewell in which I was toasted and had to give an amusing speech in reply. They presented me with an engraved pewter mug. I was sad to leave the lawyers there, many of whom were able, hardworking and great fun. But I felt I had made a contribution, in particular, in the reform of the legal aid arrangements where I had sat on policy committees and drafted successful legislation. We were very unhappy to leave Hong Kong, or the Fragrant Harbour as it was known, and never thought we might eventually return; it was a sad and final farewell. So we arranged for our Chinese furniture to be sent in a container and climbed onto the plane. As we flew west, away from the territory and into the clouds, Pam, Richard, Alexandra and I tearfully saw a Chinese junk with full, glorious brown sails gradually disappear into a tiny speck. Soon it was gone forever.

8

LORD CHANCELLOR'S DEPARTMENT 1985 – 1988

We returned to Putney in 1985 and bought a new house, an Edwardian five-bedroomed property which needed some work but was well worth it. Richard went to Donhead which was the prep school to Wimbledon College and Alexandra to the Ursuline Preparatory School also in Wimbledon. It was then that we realised Alexandra was a considerable intellectual with an exceptional memory. Richard preferred football. I returned to the Lord Chancellor's Department and was put in a corner in some office block near the Houses of Parliament and set to work on drafting new Supreme Court rules. It was about the driest and most boring task imaginable and awful in comparison to the fun and companionship of Hong Kong. Quietly, I questioned why we had returned.

I was wading through these rules when I heard there were two vacancies as assistant secretary, equivalent to captain in the Royal Navy, in the department advising the Lord Chancellor on judicial appointments. It had been decided by the permanent secretary that the boards would be on paper. I politely protested pointing out that having been in Hong Kong for four years my paper experience for the board to consider would be largely blank. Accordingly, I asked for an oral interview for all the candidates. The permanent secretary, Sir Derek Oulton, agreed. I was interviewed by a panel of three and had come very well prepared, especially in management terms. One of the panel was Derek Wiblin, a highly experienced Whitehall establishment officer, who was not afraid to speak his mind.

Luckily, I had read *In Search of Excellence*, the guru management bible of that time, and learned of the importance on Friday afternoons of 'managing by walking around' as the boss of Hewlett

Packard used to do in order to spot weaknesses. I also had clear views on the advancement of women and ethnic minorities to the bench provided they met the required standard. Still, I recognised in many cases they were not given the chance to demonstrate this. I was able to compare the legal systems of Hong Kong, New Zealand and Australia with that in England. My confidence gained by working in Hong Kong where I was a large fish in a small pond, was very useful and was recognised as such by the board.

I was then hauled before Sir Derek Oulton who gave me coffee in the House of Lords. He announced that the board had recommended me to be appointed to one of the two vacant posts. There was a long pause and then he said, looking at me squarely in the eye, 'I have long considered this recommendation and have decided to accept it.' The reluctance was palpable because he had not really seen me in action. I merely told him I would not let him down and would work long hours, get it right, do the job properly and not embarrass the Lord Chancellor or him.

I then found myself placed in a delightful office, seven pillars back from the front of the House of Lords facing Black Rod's garden. My room was Pugin-panelled with an antique clock worth many thousands of pounds ticking away above an old fashioned desk covered with red leather. I was thrilled. My predecessor, Michael Huebner, subsequently head of the court service, had left me with a small but highly efficient organisation.

Tom Legg, the deputy secretary, a distinguished ex Royal Marine commando who later became permanent secretary, came in and welcomed me before asking if I would mind carrying on putting the Public Trustee and Administration of Funds Bill through Parliament in addition to all of my new duties. I had been working on this before promotion so I was an expert on the technicalities of the office of the Public Trustee. Although it increased my workload, I naturally agreed, saying 'Aye Aye Sir', naval style.

After that I went to see the parliamentary counsel, Stephen Mason, the number four in that office in Whitehall. Having met some of the humourless administrators he decided he did not want to see any more of them and that he would deal directly with me as the lawyer on the task. This suited me but not the administrators who were trying to settle all of the policy. The first time I went to see Stephen I walked into the Office of the Parliamentary Counsel in Whitehall with my heavy brass-studded briefcase from Hong Kong. I was about to drop it down on the table in front of me but instinct prevailed. Stephen had gone white; the table was Georgian. The damage that I would have caused would have been beyond repair. The briefcase stopped an inch short of the table as I muttered something like, 'That was a near disaster. I hope that the bill does not suffer that fate.'

This bill was great fun as it was only about ten clauses. I had to take it through both Houses of Parliament including a committee where the then Conservative Attorney General led and was astute enough to ask me many questions, particularly ones I did not want to hear. But I did my best. The opposition fell into line and eventually the bill received the Royal Assent. Afterwards, we had a civilised glass of champagne and small eats in the Office of Parliamentary Counsel. Stephen Mason was a genius as far as I was concerned as he put me right and improved the drafting instructions that I had been sending him. It was a classic and lasting education in parliamentary procedure. It was about this time that Peter (later Lord) Hennessy's work *Whitehall* was published which was immensely helpful in explaining how the government worked or not as the case may be.

So I settled down into my job as the official advisor to the Lord Chancellor on all judicial appointments under the rank of circuit judge and including some at circuit judge level. These included all tribunals, stipendiary magistrates and registrars in county courts. I even arranged the appointment of the members of the inquiry to report on the MS *Herald of Free Enterprise* ferry disaster. The field was enormous. My role was to chair the boards for the candidates fronted on one side by the senior judge of that particular organisation and on the other side occasionally by a distinguished lay person who was tasked to put some common sense into what we were all trying to achieve.

The process was fair but not as thorough as the present day where written exams are called for. Even the potential Lord Chief Justice had to produce an essay on criminal justice. But then referees were produced and taken up and a detailed resume of the career of each candidate was prepared. We were well trained in interview techniques and did not ask 'What if?' questions but rather 'What did you do when…?' kind of questions. So we were looking for decisive action intellectually and practically when that particular candidate had been put into difficulties and stress. Sometimes the referees from the judiciary were not too helpful, especially when we were told that a judge was rather surprised to be asked to be a referee because he had never heard of the applicant. I was ably assisted by Stella Hutcheson, who sadly died young of breast cancer a few years later. She was the ideal foil and we worked really well as a team, backed up by the other clerical staff. It was so sad when she died with two young children left behind. She was bright, hardworking and fun and a very able lawyer.

The system is criticised nowadays as being too incestuous with officials consulting the judiciary and appointments cosily made. Now there is an independent judicial appointments authority. This advises the Lord Chancellor and the Lord Chief Justice. But, not-withstanding the appearance of a lack of independence, in 1985 every reference, letter or comment was carefully logged on highly confidential files kept on each candidate even after they had been appointed. So when promotion on the bench came around there was an up-to-date record of their achievements. We were so careful and fair and gave candidates opportunities to sit in the jurisdiction to which they aspired. Politics was largely irrelevant unless the candidate was an extremist.

I spoke to the Society of Black Lawyers and told them that on behalf of the Lord Chancellor, Lord Hailsham, I looked forward to the day when their organisation could be disbanded and did not feel such a fraternity group to be necessary. Stella spoke to the 1919 Group of Women Solicitors in a similar manner. We went out of our way to encourage ethnic minorities and female applicants. We found the latent prejudice, for example, against some women continuing even though it was disguised. In 1919 when the first female solicitors were recognised by the Law Society the first two were admitted on the same day. The Law Society Council, consisting entirely of men, decided that they must recognise the first one. But they had both been appointed on the same day. So these two female solicitors were required to run down Fleet Street. The first to arrive back at the Law Society in Chancery Lane to a cheering mob of male lawyers was declared the first female solicitor to be admitted to the Law Society. This appalling treatment did not prevail but the condescension of some male lawyers towards female ones still remained. We made due allowance for it and I am fairly sure this prejudice has largely disappeared from the legal profession today.

So from 1985 to 1988 I chaired numerous boards under great pressure to produce tribunal chairmen and women and stipendiary magistrates. We introduced a system whereby stipendiary magistrates, now called district judges, were appointed throughout the country in order to help the lay bench with cases and undertake training. This was not always well received in backwards counties because some lay members did not want some allegedly smart London lawyer in pin-striped trousers to tell them what to do. With that in mind, I introduced a system whereby potential stipendiary magistrate candidates were allowed to go to sit in the area to which they were applying so that mutual regard would soon be achieved.

At about this time, in 1986, I was sent to Northern Ireland to chair boards there for judicial appointments because Northern Ireland was at that time subject to direct rule from Westminster. I arrived in Belfast and picked my way through broken glass by the Belfast High Court – there had been a bomb attack three days earlier – to see the Lord Chief Justice of Northern Ireland, Lord Lowry who, subsequently, became a good friend. He was a wise judge and a brave man.

Some official had got wind that I was a Catholic and was obviously concerned that a 'Fenian' should not be involved in judicial appointments in Northern Ireland. He crudely asked me whether I was a 'green' Catholic or 'Downside and Ampleforth'; in other words, was I a violent supporter of Irish independence or a sound loyal fellow from a top public school? I told him in no uncertain terms that my old school had won seven Victoria Crosses and that two weeks previously with my face painted black I had been boarding ships at sea at night to protect people like him from terrorism. He did have the grace to apologise.

In one of my meetings with him I told the Lord Chief that I was much accustomed to public speaking and would be pleased to speak to a group of the Northern Ireland judiciary on behalf of the Lord Chancellor. He fixed this up after I had been around for a few days. I stood there before these judges, including High Court judges and magistrates, and reminded them that I was speaking on behalf of Lord Hailsham, the Lord Chancellor. I said I wished to pay tribute to their bravery and devotion to duty and competence in being learned in the law. The Northern Ireland Court Service headed by John Steele was a model of its kind.

I said that I knew they had bullet proof glass in the windows of their houses; that the front and back of their houses were illuminated by strong lights; that they could not go to work on a regular route; that they could not book holidays in their own names like Lord Justice Gibson, who had done just that and had been ambushed and killed on his way back from Dublin. I said they were targets for terrorists but also that they were the last line of civilised protection for people of all races and religions in Northern Ireland. They carried out their task fearlessly and without any additional financial reward. Many on the mainland did not have a clue about the stress in their lives. I continued in this vein for about fifteen minutes. It was heartfelt and genuine because I really was moved by the bravery of some of the stipendiary magistrates I had met.

The end result was that I received the nearest thing to a standing ovation I have ever had and was whisked off to the Royal Belfast Golf Club for a splendid lunch. I returned to Northern Ireland on several occasions. I was delighted by the peace that has now long prevailed in that beautiful country, which has benefitted from the devotion to duty of those brave judges and their families.

I was determined, with the instruction of the Lord Chancellor, Lord Hailsham, to seek out potential judicial candidates rather than just waiting for people to apply. As part of this initiative I visited the Birmingham Law Society and gave a lecture there about the procedure. I was then joined by my boss Tom Legg, for a formal dinner. There were over 500 present. As we were waiting to process in to the top table with a large number of distinguished people and to receive the traditional slow handclap at these kind of dinners, Tom, who was a former Royal Marines commando in National Service, muttered to me, an RNR officer, 'James, remember you are still on parade.' This was a timely and useful piece of advice which I applied then and on many subsequent occasions. While solicitors all around me were becoming more inebriated and tactless I was sipping one glass of wine and remaining quietly sober and acutely observant. It is uncanny how this friendly and useful advice, given to me by a wise public service lawyer, has stood the test of time.

It was shortly before Lord Hailsham ceased to be Lord Chancellor that I made my one and only worrying blunder. I was charged with the responsibility of finding a senior judge to run the tax tribunals in England, Wales and Scotland. This was difficult to achieve but I managed to find the right person who was a successful tax Queen's Counsel. So I produced the usual memorandum and documents for the Lord Chancellor to sign which he did four days before Christmas Eve. All was well until I received a telephone call from the clerk of the tax tribunal, an amusing chap notwithstanding the boredom of his work, who asked me whether I had seen a particular schedule to the Finance Act 1972, which amended a tax Act.

I remarked that this was bedside reading but would he be kind enough to remind me of its contents. It provided that as the appointment was also for Scotland the Scottish Lord Advocate had to be consulted. He asked me whether I had consulted the Scottish Lord Advocate about this judicial appointment. Of course I had not done so. I was unaware of the Finance Act amendment. I asked him to leave this with me. I rang the permanent secretary of the Scottish Office whom I knew who was in Whitehall. He was very helpful and sympathetic and said he would try to track down the Lord Advocate, Lord Campbell of Alloway who would sort the matter out. He indicated that there would be no need to trouble the Lord Chancellor. This whole matter could be quietly put to bed.

At Stonyhurst many years previously there had been a character-forming practice of 'reporting yourself' ordered by a senior boy where one had to report oneself to a master for appropriate punishment for some misdemeanour. This was a character test because some boys were tempted to forget to report themselves. Sometimes they got away with it but at other times there was trouble. It was a test of integrity and a character forming process too.

So I told this kind Scottish permanent secretary that I would have to report my error to the Lord Chancellor. I went to see the permanent secretary and together we went to see the Lord Chancellor. I told him what had happened and advised him that if there was a political row with the Scots about not being consulted on this judicial appointment he was to blame me for my incompetence. I described what I was doing about it which was to track down Lord Campbell of Alloway to ask him to approve this appointment. If he did I would produce another memorandum properly drafted for the Lord Chancellor to sign.

The Scottish permanent secretary did manage to track down Lord Campbell of Alloway to an obscure part of Scotland where he was on holiday. This good and kind Lord Advocate recognised my contrition and when briefed about the qualities of the judge who was to be appointed approved it at once on behalf of the Scottish establishment. I always remember him for this kindness because he could have created a frightful fuss and got me into serious trouble. I always wanted to meet him to thank him. In any event, I got the document to the Lord Chancellor on Christmas Eve. He was very grateful for the full brief and all was well.

I thought that was to be the end of it but shortly afterwards, early in the New Year, I was summoned to see the permanent secretary. I imagined it would be an interview without coffee, in service terms, where I would be given a real roasting. So I turned up nervously to find coffee laid out with some fine looking government biscuits. The permanent secretary told me he and the Lord Chancellor had been very impressed by the way I had handled the mistake I had made and the way I had kept them informed and sorted the matter out. The Lord Chancellor had asked the permanent secretary to let me know that he was pleased and relieved. He had remarked that he knew that he could trust me.

I thanked the permanent secretary for this and said that it was somewhat similar to being an officer of the watch on board a warship at night in tricky weather. The captain was in his cabin and I was on watch. However, on two occasions I requested the captain to come to the bridge because I was not happy with the conditions. Numerous tankers were trying to get into Milford Haven in a Force 7 with very poor visibility at night. There seemed to be ships all around us on the radar. The captain had come to the bridge, stayed there for half an hour and then said to me he could enjoy sound sleep from now on because he knew if there was trouble he would be called. He said I was perfectly competent to continue on my own and he retired to a deep, untroubled sleep in his pit because he trusted me. The permanent secretary was interested in this little analogy but then added the words, 'This is something in your education isn't it?' Indeed it was and I told him about the reporting oneself procedure at Stonyhurst where we were always advised to be people of integrity who could be trusted. It was a lovely moment, the finest cup of public service coffee I have ever had.

Having been in Hong Kong and been exposed to able people of different nationalities I was always fascinated by immigration problems and procedures and the question of who would be allowed entry to the UK, on what terms and how the immigration control process worked. So I was pleased when it so happened that one of my last duties with Lord Hailsham, was taking immigration adjudicators (now immigration judges) into the judicial fold.

They had been appointed by the Home Secretary notwith-standing that the Home Secretary was a party to the appeal proceedings. This didn't appear to show an impartial judiciary at work. As a result, it was decided to transfer the appointment and running of these adjudicators to the Lord Chancellor. I called on Lord Hailsham and gave him a full briefing. I said I was sure the Home Office was not transferring all the money to the Lord Chancellor's Department to meet the full cost of the transfer but there was little we could do about it. I added, 'There were no difficulties according to Home Office officials.'

Three days after the Transfer of Functions Order came into force, which I had drafted, a large brown envelope arrived on my desk. It was from the High Court. Some adjudicators had been suing the Home Secretary for perceived pension shortfalls and this formal notice decreed that on the writ 'For the Defendant, delete Secretary of State for Home Affairs and substitute, Lord High Chancellor.' Home Office officials had misled me by assuring me there were no problems!

I returned to Lord Hailsham and told him that although I had assured him a few days before that there were no problems he was now a defendant in the High Court! Lord Hailsham, still treat-ing me as a favourite grandson, was most understanding and told me to resist this action and keep him informed. Subsequently, I addressed the assembled adjudicators, about forty in total, some of whom I thought were unnecessarily pompous and hostile to me personally. I told them they were no longer civil servants but responsible members of the judiciary and whatever the merits or otherwise of their pension dispute they were getting an immediate pay rise of £10,000. I urged them to act responsibly, abandon their action on pensions and 'join the judicial family'. All except four did. These four were supported in their court action by a civil service union, who eventually abandoned them altogether. The issue quietly disappeared. Little did I realise then that I would become one of their number.

In early 1987 the Lord Chancellor, Lord Hailsham retired and was replaced by Lord Havers who was only Lord Chancellor for a short time and retired on ill-health grounds. He was succeeded by Lord Mackay, a Scottish law lord. He was a most interesting and brilliant man who had been a lecturer in mathematics before he took up the law. He was always so courteous and thoughtful and had an intellect to match. I remain very respectful and fond of him. On one occasion he was being given a brief on the budget by senior officials in the department; as an official was droning on, Lord Mackay glanced at the figures and, with his mathematical skill looked up and said, 'I think they add up to 105 per cent.' He was right. The red faced official was asked to go away and come back with figures which amounted to 100 per cent.

Work in the department steadily increased and I found myself cycling into the House of Lords from Putney on Saturdays and sometimes even Sundays. On Saturday mornings I would work for about three hours and then have a coffee with Tom Legg who was always there. I learned much from him about how Whitehall operated. The work was exhilarating. I really enjoyed being in the House of Lords because, as I walked down the red-carpeted corridors, I saw figures from the past who had been hugely important at one time or other but were now somehow forgotten or diminished.

So many politicians were much smaller in real life than they had appeared on television.

We were allowed to use the library in the House of Lords where incredibly heavy cast iron ladders were used to retrieve books from high shelves. I was always worried that in trying to move one of these ladders I would lose control and manage to cause serious injury to some distinguished old snoring peer in a deep red leather chair. We were also allowed to use the main Lords dining room on Fridays, when nearly all the peers were absent. It was fun eating there but the food was truly grim.

On one occasion I managed to obtain a ticket for my mother to sit in the gallery reserved for duchesses to watch proceedings in the House of Lords. This was kindly organised by the private office. My mother had a wonderful time, followed by a pleasant tea. Pam and I went to several garden parties at Buckingham Palace, where the catering and organisation were most impressive. But we were not important enough to be chosen to meet the Queen.

The judicial appointments office was small and everyone worked fiendishly hard to be fair and considerate. I used to carry out pastoral duties. When an applicant had not been successful or wanted a move I would do my best to be kind, constructive and helpful. Sometimes I was involved in advising the Lord Chancellor where some judge had carried out a misdemeanour like being involved in a punch up in a rugby club or had been caught drink driving. I was always struck by the penitence of those people who had misbehaved. All the Lord Chancellors I served were compassionate in these circumstances, with one exception: dishonesty. If that person had been dishonest, he or she would be required to resign. I recall only one such case which itself indicated that the judicial appointments system worked well.

Regularly I worked to 10 p.m. On one occasion, being rather tired and as the House of Lords canteen had long closed, I walked down to the House of Commons canteen and bought a large mug of coffee in a green House of Commons plastic cup. I was proceeding back to my office when from out of the shadows pounced a uniformed doorkeeper of the Lords staff, a former sergeant major. 'You cannot carry that there coffee in 'ere down this corridor,' he barked. I was tired and unwisely tried sarcasm. 'Do you really think the Lord Chancellor cares that this is, God help us, a House of Commons coffee and would like me to fall flat on my antique desk with exhaustion and spike my face with the Victorian envelope opener which graces it?'

I found myself followed by the Deputy Black Rod, silk stockings, buckle shoes, sword, medals and all. I quickened my pace and when I turned a corner, I ran. I really ran. He never found me. But the next day the amusing private secretary to the Lord Chancellor, Richard Stoate, sent round a note to a few of us likely suspects. I owned up and dear Richard sent a soothing apology to which I joined, so all was well.

In 1987 Susie was born. We had intended to name her Tom after my generous and understanding boss. But she was a girl so we called her by the fine Biblical name of Susannah. I admitted to Pam years later that I wanted to call her Susannah after Susannah York, the actress, with whom I was besotted. In any event Susie settled on Susie so it didn't matter.

One day the permanent secretary came into my office and said it had been decided I should extend my management skills from managing a team of about ten to be the chief executive of the Royal Courts of Justice in The Strand and the probate service in England and Wales. I was being asked to run the largest court complex in Europe! So it was that early in 1988 I found myself in a dingy office in the Royal Courts of Justice having had a delightful but rather sad farewell party in the House of Lords.

9

ROYAL COURTS OF JUSTICE
1988 – 1991

As soon as I heard the news that instead of running a team of about ten I would be in charge of 1,500, I realised that the management courses I had attended in the Lord Chancellor's Department were going to be wholly inadequate. These largely consisted of lectures with someone using a flip chart and asking questions like, 'What is meant by leadership?' Everyone would then contribute their little piece such as competence, confidence, knowledge of the subject and patience. These would be solemnly written down on the flip chart. A tree would appear and everyone would leave suitably impressed by the diagram and its bubbles and interlocking branches. Those who could produce bubble diagrams like this were highly regarded and promoted. Nothing would have been remembered the following morning by any of the trainees. But it had been a day off work.

Acutely aware of the gaps in my knowledge, I installed myself for a week at a hotel in Norfolk to take a course, *The One Minute Manager*, invented by a guru called Ken Blanchard and run by an American management company. It was utterly brilliant. I was instructed how to manage a large organisation and, in particular, to draw up business plans including critical success factors so that success could be measured and failure identified.

Armed with the knowledge and notes I had acquired on the course, as well as a report on the Northern Ireland Court Service by the Cranfield Management School, I arrived at the Royal Courts of Justice in the Strand to be shown to my dingy office on the third floor. I had no personal staff at all apart from a charming female secretary who was very elderly and dying of cancer. She could not work an electric typewriter. She had to use a manual typewriter as though we were in an undertaker's office in the 1930s. It was that depressing.

I made my number with the somewhat suspicious senior judiciary because previous managers had tended to be of the forelock touching mentality; I breezed in confident and determined, knowing like Cecil Rhodes that there was much to do and little time to do it in. I asked for a business plan and there wasn't one. There was just a budget which had been grossly exceeded with a running cost deficit that had to be paid back. All the many departments in the law courts such as Chancery dealing with trusts, land problems and taxation and Queen's Bench dealing with personal injuries and civil disputes, the Commercial Court and the Family Court and the Court of Appeal, all seemed to work entirely independently of each other. They had no regard for the needs and expertise elsewhere. Still, it all just about worked in a muddled way because the court staff had been there for very many years and had become experts. There was virtually no security at all.

I realised this was going to be a daunting task. For a while I worked for a full seven days every week sorting problems out. My first task was to move myself into decent accommodation at the centre of the action in the old Attorney General's office with two secretaries, an excellent personal assistant and good immediate staff. I then formed a management board consisting of senior clerks of the various divisions and the accommodation officer, the renowned Doug Noon, and finance officer Keith Fairweather, who was highly numerate and competent on spread sheets. I also recruited highly experienced listing officers (who prepare the list of cases each day) from courts all over London including the Old Bailey.

It was apparent that many targets had been set years before which were largely ignored. Ancient Dickensian clerks in the bankruptcy court, for example, were recording obscure procedures under section 127 of an obsolete Act which were of no use to anyone. *Bleak House* was constantly on my mind. After three months I produced a comprehensive business plan for the whole of the law courts with fifty-five targets to be met in various places such as processing writs on time. The progress on meeting those targets was carefully monitored.

During that time I also had some fun with the senior judges on targeted work. Master of the Rolls Lord Donaldson, the senior civil appeal judge, said to me I should work for the judiciary and to the judiciary, that is to say I should be responsible to them. I replied I would work and did work for the judiciary seven days a week but not to the judiciary because I was responsible to the Lord Chancellor. If I worked to the judiciary, they would be responsible for the budget I had secured and therefore answerable to Parliament for how that budget was spent. In this way judges would be sucked into parliamentary scrutiny and their independence might have been prejudiced. I got on well with Lord Donaldson as he was a keen sailor.

The Lord Chief Justice was the formidable Geoffrey Lane AFC, a bomber pilot in World War II and his deputy was Lord Justice Tasker Watkins, who had won the Victoria Cross in 1944. They were a powerful duo who looked upon me with a degree of caution. They were concerned I was somehow or other going to tread on the toes of judicial independence. So I engineered a meeting with the senior judiciary and explained to them in clear terms that I recognised where the boundary lay between administration and the judiciary, a clear line in the sand, and that I would not cross it. If I did purport to cross it, I would expect to be advised by them – hopefully politely. I emphasised that I was there to help them, to work in partnership and to make the operation in this huge Victorian building of 1,500 rooms more effective, efficient and safe.

When I asked the staff what the security was in the building, I discovered there were just five cameras pointing outwards at various entrances to the building. The cameras were only showing the black shadow of someone entering or leaving. The scenes they monitored were not even recorded.

Springing to action, I telephoned Heathrow, spoke to the security chief there and invited him to check me out. Three days later I turned up with a team of experts whom I had recruited. We were warmly welcomed by the extremely efficient security team at Heathrow. Shortly after this, security arches and traveller luggage security machines similar to those used at Heathrow were delivered to the law courts and installed. They were leased because they were too expensive to buy.

Then I had some more fun. I invited the senior judiciary to come down to the main entrance to the law courts, where 2,000 members of the public and lawyers entered between 9 a.m. and 10 a.m., and were barely checked by security. I gave the judiciary a demonstration of the new machine. Various law books were put on the moving traveller and one of them was a hollowed out copy of *Archbold: Criminal Pleading, Evidence and Practice* into which we had inserted Semtex. This came through the machine bright orange. I informed the judges that this proved the machine worked because that was Semtex. When I had retrieved the panicking judiciary from all four corners of the main hall, I explained that it was actually benign. They were impressed, if sheepishly irritated by me.

When I asked the staff who cleaned the judges' rooms I got the simple answer, 'Cleaners, James!' It then emerged that these were unchecked individuals, probably illegal immigrants, who were cleaning the judges' rooms at 5 a.m. entirely unsupervised. This included the room of the Lord Chief Justice. I was flabbergasted and called in the owner of the business who supplied the cleaners. I invited him to nominate six individuals who would be security checked. They were the only people allowed to clean the judges' rooms. They would also be under the supervision of the permanent staff at 6 a.m. This arrangement worked well.

As a result of all this I finally received the trust of the judiciary; they realised that, actually, I could be rather helpful to them and they were just as appalled by the lack of security as I was. By the time I left three years later there was a sophisticated security system with fifty cameras around the building, all operated from a command centre which began to look like the cockpit of Concorde. I was involved in installing many other security measures which would not be appropriate to disclose in this book because they continue to be in use today. Suffice to say, the security is still very impressive.

After this, I raised the question as to when the last fire drill had taken place in the law courts and was given an answer, somewhere in about 1923. I decided another drill was needed. In order to mitigate the effect on the efficiency of the court proceedings, I chose to have it around the main hall as it would affect only about fifteen courts. Each judge would be warned in advance. The fire drill would take place at 12.45 p.m. so they would all have fifteen minutes extra for lunch in the Middle Temple. In this way, I managed to persuade the reluctant but hungry judges to cooperate.

The great day came and the tannoy system announced, 'Fire, fire, fire. Please evacuate the courts and assemble on The Strand.' But there was an electrical fault. The tannoy system designed to warn people in the main hall and judges in those courts when there was a fire drill, didn't work. Yet, the tannoy in another part of the law courts where judges and staff were totally unprepared and didn't know anything about this fire drill, did work. There was a fault on the switch board. Panic! It was a real shambles and people were falling over themselves to get out of the building. It was like the Calgary Stampede. This persuaded the senior judiciary that, indeed, the system needed proper testing. By the time I left, fire drills were very effectively being carried out every three months.

Throughout my time at the Royal Courts of Justice, I still had to cope with unnecessary interference from some members of the judiciary who considered themselves to be all knowing about matters unconnected with the law. At that time the new Thomas More building, consisting of thirteen floors, was being built; I thought the work was going well but had taken my eye off the ball. Each floor had a judge's room, a clerk's room, a loo and a court room.

When the first floor of the Thomas More building had been completed there was a demonstration.

Enter from stage left the Lord Chief Justice, the Master of the Rolls, senior Lords Justices, High Court judges and other terribly important people. The Lord Chief Justice noticed that the bench on which the judges would sit was rather high so he went into the judge's room and found himself walking up a mini spiral staircase. As he walked along behind the chairs to sit down on the judge's chair, he nearly scraped his head on the ceiling. Then he called for someone to go into the witness box. He soon announced that he could not see the person in the witness box because the bench was too high. The rim of the judge's desk interfered with the line of sight to the person who was in the witness box which was far too low below him. I was asked pretty curtly what had gone wrong. Amused and superior eyes glanced haughtily at me. I replied I had no idea that the bench had been moved so high. I would investigate.

Then a Lord Justice, who had better remain nameless, but who has since died, put up his hand. He announced in a soft voice that he had directed the civil engineers to raise the bench because he thought it would be appropriate for the judges to sit high up gazing down upon the assembled people below. As such, he had ordered a change in the specification without informing me. Still, they all looked to me for a solution.

Being a practising Christian I immediately knew what was required: a pulpit. Each court is now fitted with a pulpit for the witness with a small spiral staircase so the witness could be seen at a higher level by the judges. The building itself was late in completion, but not by much. There were penalty clauses in the contract which led a director of this renowned international civil engineering company to come and see me. He said that part of the reason for the delay was the change in specification by the judiciary. I waived the penalty clauses and we had a drink together. The opening of this striking building was very successful.

At times the responsibility of being the chief executive of the law courts was rather like that of a Home Secretary as described by Roy Jenkins. It is being able to deal with a thunderbolt which comes out of a clear blue sky on a Monday morning. On one occasion I came in to find that a disgruntled and probably ill member of staff had been in the courts on a Sunday. He had collected numerous documents, including pleadings and cheques, put them into bin bags and had set the whole lot alight. This had to be sorted out by going back to the solicitors and inviting them to submit the papers again. The judges kindly granted an extension of time for all this to happen. It took some sorting out.

I soon found that this member of staff was not going to be sacked but would be given some leave and then allowed to return. I put my foot down and declared that I owed a responsibility to people who worked in the law courts. I did not mind if he was retired on medical grounds but certainly he would not be allowed back at all to work there. So that was that.

I then somewhat unwisely called in the Bar and the Law Society for a meeting so they could tell me in their view how improvements could be made at the law courts. The universal view was that the queues for the submissions of documents like pleadings and grounds of appeal and writs and cheques were taking far too long to move. It was costing Barristers' Chambers and solicitors unnecessary money for them to pay staff to stand in a queue for ages waiting for some member of staff to put down their cup of coffee and deal with the proceedings.

I visited the Queen's Bench Division to watch what happened; I found some members of staff working but not always going up to the counter to deal with the long queue. Also, and more significantly, people in the queue hadn't a clue what they were supposed to be doing. There were people there in motor-cycle helmets with brown envelopes on which was written 'Bill – Stick this into court. They will tell you what to do.' So part of the time was spent by the staff in correcting forms and trying to help the poor outdoor clerks, as they were called, do their duty. Then I recalled the Bar and the Law Society with my detailed findings. Somewhat rashly I told them, that in order to be helpful, I would produce Supreme Court checklists to help members of the legal profession. This proposal was gratefully received.

For the next four months and with the assistance of the clerks in each of the divisions I produced a published information booklet, describing for example: issuing a writ or summons and what was required on the form, when foreign currency should be converted into pounds, where the documents should be sent and who should sign them. There were examples of the correct completion of such documents and instructions on how many copies were required. In many of these cases there had been difficulties where incorrect fees had been paid or only one copy had been produced.

These check-lists were provided for the Admiralty and Commercial Courts, the Chancery Division, the Court of Appeal Civil Division, the Family Division, the Queen's Bench Division and the Companies Court. I had this document published and then put up for sale for a fairly nominal fee. It proved to be a bestseller; several thousand were snapped up by the legal profession in London and, indeed, around the country. The Lord Chancellor, Mackay, was very grateful for this but the effort in producing it was exhausting. I am glad to say a similar document is still used today.

There had been some success, but I still had to solve the problem over the running cost debt. My predecessors had kept permanent civil service numbers down in accordance with government directives but then approached Job Centres in order to employ part-time workers. It was like something out of *Yes Minister*. The number of permanent staff had indeed been reduced to meet political targets, but at added cost. It was an amusing farce to others but not to me who had to sort the mess out. I had to pick up the pieces. There was a considerable debt.

I soon found out that part of the Family Division was occupying an office block near Trafalgar Square and was due to return to join the rest of the Family Division in Somerset House, for which I was also responsible, in six months' time. The six months' rent was broadly equivalent to the debt in the running costs budget. Therefore, I ordered the lease to be terminated and for the staff to move at once to Somerset House thus saving six months' rent. Then a functionary in headquarters told me that, as this was an accommodation matter, the money saved from leaving this office block early should go to headquarters and not to my budget. I responded by saying that this senior functionary should therefore go to the Lord Chief Justice to explain to him why he was not going to have so many staff and judges to meet the backlog of cases. This caused an instant change of heart! The budget was secured and the Lord Chief retained his judges and staff.

By this time the business plan was working. Whenever there was a surge of work in bankruptcy or in the Companies Court, for example, I was able to identify and quantify it in order to deploy staff with lighter loads from elsewhere in the building. They were able to help the staff who were overburdened. The staff and the judiciary began to see that having a unified business plan for the law courts was actually a help rather than a hindrance. I began to have a very good relationship with the Lord Chief Justice of whom I became very fond and fiercely loyal. We worked as a team.

Many distinguished people came in and out of the building. I managed to institute a warning system so that in appropriate cases I could meet them. For example, we had a number of visitors as part of the Anglo-American Legal Exchange which encouraged renowned judges, professors and advocates to visit each other's jurisdictions. Three Supreme Court Justices from the United States and various professors and judges numbering about fifteen in total were to be shown around the law courts by the renowned Lord Bridge, a law lord. I invited them into my chambers for coffee and government biscuits, to give them a little introduction and welcome.

At the end of my very short speech I said I hoped they would be able to ignore the words of the American humourist, Will Rodgers, who observed, 'The Americans have never lost a war, but never won a conference.' I said I very much hoped this would be the exception on this occasion. It was not very funny, but the sort of remark where a polite chuckle is the normal way to behave. The Americans, of course, looked at me with silent, stony faces. At the back Lord Bridge kindly produced the statutory laugh.

I organised for them to visit various court rooms. Lord Denning who was then the Master of the Rolls just before he retired was briefed. These judges trooped into court with much inclining of the necks from them and Lord Denning. He then impressively summed up the case he was hearing saying this side is saying that, that side is saying this; if this side says that it will lose, if the other side establishes that it will win and all the rest of it. It was a masterly demonstration of intellect and judicial ability which was most impressive. Then I took them to hear Mr Justice Hirst give an extempore judgment in the Commercial Court. After witnessing the argument for about half an hour between two counsel he gave his judgment entirely without notes; it was quite brilliant. The Americans could not believe it and asked where the research staff were and who had written his speech. I said this was the way it happened in England. The judges were selected for their intellectual calibre and judgment and ability to dispose of the work efficiently, fairly and effectively. They were hugely impressed.

In 1989 the Children Act came into force. This involved many children having to come to court in Somerset House, a magnificent listed building by the Thames. This was part of my responsibility. I inspected the place and noticed the iron balustrades supporting the railings on the stairs were set wide apart. Little Kevin, with his face covered in tomato ketchup, might fall through the balustrades to certain death three floors below. The blame would be on me! I instructed the staff to reduce the distance between the balustrades by inserting temporary ones, only to be met by an obstinate refusal from English Heritage. There was a row as I tried to argue that an allowance should be made for those working there in, as it were, a living building. But they would not budge. So I did not know what to do and was given no help by a willing but unimaginative staff.

Two days later I went off to Lords to a Test match which included watching the players practising in the nets in the Nursery ground. It was then that I had a brainwave; a rather rare occurrence for me. I instructed the staff to order a supply of cricket nets and had them suspended horizontally between floors. Kevin would be safe. The balustrades had been preserved but the place looked appalling. English Heritage did not mind as they pointed out accurately that the Family Division would one day move out of there. So the fine ornate stairs would be – and were – preserved. We were both right.

Late in 1990 the permanent secretary did a formal inspection with his team of the law courts. I had a full report with facts and figures, budget and security. The report described the disposal of business and the operation of the administration, including building work. He was kind enough to say I had transformed the law courts and the culture of its management. It was a testing time but I learned to respect the ability and hard work of the senior judiciary and noted that the higher they climbed the less pompous they became. It was only some of the junior judiciary who got the dreaded 'judgitis' and became pompous and insufferable, speaking with a slow strangulated voice. Later I remembered this and tried not to be so insufferable on the bench myself.

One day I noticed in the chambers of the senior master of the Queen's Bench Division and Admiralty Registrar, Keith Topley, a fine photograph of his boat wearing the White Ensign. I remarked that I had not realised he was a member of the Royal Yacht Squadron. He replied that the photograph had been there for ten years and I was the first so-and-so to notice it. He was understanding then when I informed him that owing to cuts the masters would have to make their own tea! The lovely elderly ladies with the tea trolleys and jam biscuits were a tradition of the past.

The work continued. It was exhausting; partly, I suspect, because I did not delegate enough. Then one day late in 1990 the phone rang and it was David Edwards, CMG, the law officer in Hong Kong responsible for legal advice on the handover of Hong Kong to China. He was a former deputy legal advisor at the Foreign Office and vastly experienced. He was looking for a deputy in Hong Kong and he offered me the job at a greatly increased salary and terms to the ones in England. I was interested, but I knew it would be unlikely I would be allowed to return to Hong Kong by the senior officials in the Lord Chancellor's Department.

So I mentioned about six names of people I knew around Whitehall who would be ideally suited to the job. He declared that most of these names were already on his list. I remarked that it appeared he was not offering me the job, merely offering me the opportunity to join a relatively long list. I added that, if for one reason or another he was unable to attract any of them, it was open to him to return to me. A week later I received a phone call from David who said two of the main candidates didn't want the job. One had labradors in Wiltshire and another would miss his fox hunting. There was no hunting in Hong Kong. He offered me the job and we agreed he should come to our house in Putney with his wife whom Pam entertained. I had a formal interview with David and we got along famously.

When I raised this move with the personnel people at headquarters and the permanent secretary I was told I already had the opportunity to get a decent suntan and couldn't be spared. I was then flattered by the establishment officer, who told me the department had it in mind to promote me to under-secretary, equivalent to rear admiral, to run a circuit of courts in the north. I found out that there would be a pay rise of only about £3,000 for this, whereas the job in Hong Kong as deputy legal advisor offered a small fortune, by my standards.

Cleverly, David managed to engineer it so that a minister at the Foreign Office telephoned the Lord Chancellor and said I was needed especially to establish the Court of Final Appeal in Hong Kong. With some reluctance, I was released up to 1997, when the handover of Hong Kong to China was due to take place.

Before I left I delivered a farewell speech to the Lord Chief, senior judiciary and staff and invited them all out to Hong Kong, provided they didn't all come at once. The Lord Chief presented me with a framed picture of the law courts. I handed over to my successor, secured the opportunity to return to the Lord Chancellor's Department in writing and prepared to return to Hong Kong. It was an exciting time.

I like to think I left the law courts in a far better state than I found them. I certainly managed to secure a much more equal relationship between senior members of the staff there and the judiciary. I had introduced a newsletter which was received by everyone so that they could see where the problems lay and what was being done about them. Senior members of the judiciary realised that the staff could actually be really helpful to them if given the opportunity. I left with a lasting and permanent respect for the intellectual ability, fairness and sheer hard work of the senior judiciary. Seven years later, when I was appointed a judge in 1998, I tried to follow the example set by these impressive people, especially when I sat in the law courts myself.

10

HONG KONG: A BRIEF HISTORY

I arrived in Hong Kong at an interesting time; after decades of disputes between the UK and China, the sovereignty of the Hong Kong territory was about to be transferred from one to the other. It was a once in a lifetime event; preceded by conflicts going back more than 100 years.

During the early nineteenth century British traders, especially from the East India Company, had traded through Canton and other Chinese coastal ports. The British brought in opium and ruthlessly traded it for silver and tea. Eventually these arrangements broke down. The Chinese government had a sense of humour failure; they burned down the warehouses containing the opium. In response, the British sent in naval frigates which were far more powerful than the blunt-bowed Chinese fighting junks.

Captain Charles Elliot was then sent to wrangle with the weakened Chinese government. He negotiated receipt of Hong Kong causing the great British Foreign Secretary of the time, Lord Palmerston, to utter the immortal rebuke, 'Hong Kong is a barren rock with scarcely a house upon it.' The negotiations resulted in the Treaty of Nanking in 1842, which gave Hong Kong Island in perpetuity to the UK. After more fighting, the southern part of the Kowloon peninsula followed, also in perpetuity, by the Convention of Peking in 1860. The rest of the territory of Hong Kong, comprising ninety-two per cent of the total land area, was leased to the British for ninety-nine years from 1 July 1898 by the second Convention of Peking.

It was extraordinary how both main races, Europeans and Chinese, had looked down on each other. To some Europeans the Chinese made ideal workers and *amahs* or formal maids. No

Chinese were allowed to own a house on the Peak until as late as 1972. While I was out there I would occasionally lunch in the mess of the Hong Kong Regiment run by British officers on secondment. I had to hand in my bill to the so-called 'No. 1 Boy' who was about eighty-two years old and incidentally the sweetest man ever.

The Chinese in Hong Kong looked down on the foreigners or *gweilos* as barbarians from the outer kingdom. It was worse if the foreigner had a beard or was unruly and hairy. Even the boat boys would smirk with derision at the pink-faced and sweaty European women as they stumbled on board a junk for a picnic in Repulse Bay. One leading firm of London solicitors honestly named their junk ship *Tau Ting*.

But by the time I arrived for my second stint in Hong Kong, the pendulum had swung. Money talks. Massively wealthy entrepreneurs like Li Ka Shing and sophisticated multi-lingual Chinese really ran the place in business terms, although the old Hongs like Jardines and Swires were successful, sophisticated and wealthy.

It used to be cynically observed that Hong Kong was run by the Jockey Club, the Bank and the governor, in that order. Indeed more money would be put on one afternoon's racing in Hong Kong than all the races and racecourses in England for a year. The race courses at Sha Tin and Happy Valley were state of the art places run with the latest technology. Another difference was that inter-racial marriages were happily regarded as normal. It was mainly European men marrying beautiful and elegant Chinese girls. There were some immensely distinguished and wealthy Anglo Chinese families like the Hotungs who were noted charity benefactors.

The educated Chinese had one significant advantage. They spoke the two strands of Chinese; Cantonese (spoken locally in Hong Kong) and Mandarin. Very few Europeans could master the language. About 5,000 characters had to be mastered even to read a newspaper. Misunderstandings abounded. My colleagues would break out into Cantonese if they did not want me to understand.

One day I was late for a meeting with senior people. I strode in, apologised for being late and remarked by way of explanation, 'Badgers on the line at Oxshott,' a quote from *The Fall and Rise of Reginald Perrin* by David Nobbs. The English all laughed but the Chinese sat silently convinced more than ever that I was indeed a barbarian and an eccentric one too.

One consistent feature of Hong Kong life was the presence of the well organised British forces, mainly the Royal Navy and the Army with a small RAF element. The Army was mainly engaged in border security with the Gurkhas prominent. The navy patrol ships also engaged in maritime safety across the South China Sea.

On the whole the British forces were well disciplined but there were lapses. When I was there two Scottish soldiers well-oiled from booze stole a rifle and a Land Rover from the base in Stanley. At 3 a.m. they drove through Wanchai singing Scottish ballads tunelessly, while shooting up windows in tall buildings. Mercifully no one was hurt. Next they holed up at the airport and shot out a clock. They refused to surrender. Soon a young British Royal Hong Kong policeman arrived and announced that he had just been on the course for hostage situations. He was given the megaphone and with great tension asked, 'What are your demands?' It was expected that these would include a flight to a South Sea Island, some money and security out of there. But back came the reply, 'A packet of fags and a pint of Tetleys please.' This was not in the course script. They eventually surrendered and were bundled out of Hong Kong to serve a tough sentence at home.

The government of China had always regarded the British occupation of Hong Kong as somehow illegal. Chinese leaders through the 1960s and 1970s said that China would 'resume the exercise of sovereignty' in its own good time. But a lease was a lease. The British with their scrupulous attention to detail and respect for the letter of the law never denied that the lease of ninety-two per cent of Hong Kong would cease on 1 July 1997.

At that time there was increasing concern in Hong Kong about the expiry of leases of land in the New Territories and the financial consequences for mortgages and investments and, indeed, for contracts which straddled 1997. The negotiators, organised by the Foreign Office, included Sir Murray MacLehose, the governor. He was a typical Foreign Office product, a bright and apparently arrogant aristocrat. Still, he was a good Mandarin speaker and, although a bureaucrat himself, he had little time for the officials of the Hong Kong government, especially its lawyers who, at that time, largely consisted of loud Australian prosecutors with a liking for long liquid lunches. A British team was assembled including Sir Percy Cradock, then British Ambassador to Beijing. The Chinese side was led by Deng Xiaoping, diminutive, chain-smoking and very bright.

Margaret Thatcher, the British Prime Minister, went to China in September 1982. There was a formal meeting with the Chinese Prime Minister Zhao Ziyang in the Great Hall of the People where she announced the British government had a moral obligation to the people of Hong Kong, arguing that after 1997 Hong Kong should remain a British administration. Without British backing, she said, Hong Kong would surely collapse. After the meeting was over, Thatcher fell down the steps of the Great Hall of The People. The Chinese saw this as a bad omen for the negotiations and proof of a fundamental weakness in the British position!

The next day Thatcher met Deng Xiaoping. He launched straight in, stating that China would resume sovereignty in 1997. There would be negotiations which must not last longer than two years or China would impose its own solution. The temperature was then lowered and a communiqué was issued; talks through diplomatic channels would take place with the common aim of maintaining the way of life and prosperity of Hong Kong.

The negotiations eventually started, the British diplomatic team led by the brilliant Sir Percy Cradock. In his team were the usual crop of Foreign Office bright young diplomats including Anthony Galsworthy, a direct descendant of the novelist, and William Ehrman, an old Etonian, both of whom subsequently became the ambassadors in Beijing; and Robert Peirce and Nigel Inkster. All were good Mandarin speakers.

One of the standard negotiating ploys of the Chinese government is to erect a principle or a number of them before the talks start. These principles are actually in many cases the Chinese objective for the talks. So if they are accepted all that is left to talk about is the implementation of these Chinese objectives disguised as principles. The game is lost before the referee has blown his whistle for the kick off. The way to proceed is for both sides quietly to acknowledge without saying so that they have a different interpretation of the principles. This process of riding off the Chinese from their principles can be a long and time consuming struggle.

Quite quickly it was obvious the talks were leading nowhere and the British side became concerned. Thankfully, Sir Percy Cradock, with his knowledge of the Chinese mind and negotiating tactics, deftly switched the talks away from the principle of sovereignty to administrative arrangements to safeguard the Hong Kong people. The Hong Kong public didn't know that in practice Britain had given up on sovereignty after 1997. They didn't know that in effect the whole territory was going back to China. The British government then suggested to the Chinese side that there should be a treaty enshrining the new arrangements. This was effective and in November 1983 the Chinese started serious discussions on the terms of such a document.

At this time the Chinese feared the British would run off with the assets of Hong Kong or drain the finances so that there would be little left in the Treasury in 1997. With this mind, they suggested creating a commission to oversee the last years of British administration. This caused a row in the talks as it looked like Chinese interference in British administration before the handover. In order to speed things up, Sir Percy Cradock, who had by then retired from the Foreign Office but was still heavily involved back in the UK, decided to set up a drafting team to work in Beijing with the Chinese side. David Wilson, who subsequently became the governor of Hong Kong, was appointed to lead this talented drafting team.

There were issues like the legal system, judicial appointments, international treaties, civil aviation and the minefield of land law, especially New Territories leases. There was also trouble over passports. Eventually, after detailed negotiations lasting long into the night on many occasions, the terms of the Sino-British Joint Declaration on the Question of Hong Kong, a genuine international treaty, was initialled by the two sides in the Great Hall of the People. In my view it was a testament to, and a triumph for, Foreign and Commonwealth Office diplomatic and drafting skills.

The basic deal was that China would resume the exercise of sovereignty over all of Hong Kong, including the bits given in perpetuity, on 1 July 1997. Hong Kong would on that day become part of China. Responsibility for foreign affairs and defence of Hong Kong would be passed to China. In return China agreed that the Hong Kong Special Administrative Region (HKSAR) would enjoy a high degree of autonomy. The current social, economic and legal systems in Hong Kong would remain unchanged for fifty years and private property, ownership of enterprises, rights of inheritance and foreign investment would continue to be protected by law.

Freedom of speech, of the person, of the press, of assembly, of religion, of the right to join trade unions and of travel were all protected. All this is well summed up in the provision of the Joint Declaration which states that the previous capitalist system and lifestyle of Hong Kong shall remain unchanged for fifty years. This sort of colourful language is unusual for an international treaty but it demonstrates well the ingenious concept of 'one country, two systems' coined by the late Deng Xiaoping.

Under the Joint Declaration a Joint Liaison Group (JLG) was established. This consisted of diplomats from the UK, China and the Hong Kong government. Its function was to conduct consultation on the implementation of the Joint Declaration and to discuss matters relating to the smooth transfer of government in 1997. When I arrived in 1991 I was one of the legal advisors to the British side. Then, when David Edwards left Hong Kong in 1995, I became the legal advisor on site representing in effect both the Hong Kong Government and the Foreign Office.

11

RETURN TO HONG KONG:
1991 – 1997

In the room where the JLG met to discuss the transfer of government there was a long table with microphones and flowers. If it was cold outside one leader was bound to say the warmer air inside was conducive to warm relations and good progress. If it was warm outside but cold inside the leader would say he was bringing the warm air in for the purposes of a warm atmosphere for successful negotiations. Both leaders were temporarily lost for words when the air-conditioning at one meeting leaked drops of water on their heads until somebody observed that the water would help them keep cool under pressure.

All the officials knew each other well so even when there were disagreements and the language was firm, no one was insulting or rude. The Chinese spoke in Mandarin, which was interpreted into English and the British spoke in English translated into Mandarin, though many members of both sides spoke both languages. My task was to help implement the international law aspects of the Joint Declaration as the deputy to the former Foreign Office Legal Advisor, David Edwards.

I got to know the lawyers from China well. They were able, dedicated and internationally trained. The British side was equally well-equipped; it was a well-oiled machine. The JLG met about four times a year in plenary session in Beijing, London and Hong Kong. Its expert groups met almost continuously. The achievements of the JLG, many of them in areas of international law, were significant. The work was extremely complex; Hong Kong was a separate contracting party under what is now known as the World Trade Organisation and it was allowed to participate in thirty other international organisations either in its own right or as a member of the sovereign government delegation. These included the International Maritime Organisation, World Health Organisation and Interpol.

On one occasion I was the sole Hong Kong representative at a Joint International Maritime Organisation/UN Conference on shipping law, held in Geneva. I arrived at the Palais des Nations in Geneva to find myself seated at a huge horse-shoe shaped table with about 170 other parties present. The great moment came when it was my turn to speak so I pressed the red button and the light came on. The chairman said, 'Distinguished delegate from Hong Kong.' I then gave my six or seven minute speech on technical matters which had been carefully prepared beforehand.

Immediately after this another red button went on and the chairman said, 'Distinguished delegate from the Russian Federation.' The Russian delegate then said, 'Having heard the distinguished delegate from Hong Kong, we in the Russian delegation have now changed our mind.' On went my red button and the chairman said, 'Distinguished delegate from Hong Kong.' I observed, 'The distinguished delegate from the Russian Federation has not indicated how he has changed his mind, whether he approved of my arguments or found them sadly unacceptable.' There were ripples of laughter when the Russian delegate said he had changed his mind in favour of my position.

I was then on the inside track. I had made my mark. I was invited to join the drafting committee of lawyers from around the world led by an amazing former East German lawyer, whose name I have forgotten, in her thirties, who was fluent in six languages. We all adored her. We worked hard and well together. When, after one month, we all had to say goodbye having drafted this treaty, many of us were in tears because we knew we would never see each other again. I imagine she is an ambassador somewhere now.

The basic work of the International Law Division in Hong Kong was to persuade the Chinese side to agree that membership of international organisations and treaties which had been applied to Hong Kong by the British government could continue in force for the Hong Kong government while under Chinese sovereignty. Unique and difficult problems of international law were grasped. David Edwards was remarkable in his ability to change international law. For example, there were some treaties like the International Covenant on Civil and Political Rights, a worldwide international treaty, which applied to Hong Kong by virtue of British sovereignty but to which the Chinese were not a party at all. So we managed to secure agreement that these and similar treaties could continue to apply in Hong Kong after the handover but under Chinese sovereignty. China would remain responsible for continuing to implement them.

No one wanted Hong Kong to be a haven for international crooks so we negotiated and signed a series of surrender of fugitive offender and extradition agreements. These were bilateral agreements. When negotiating one of these agreements with the United States, I ran into trouble. I was leading on the talks and had to explain to a very large gentleman from the State Department, in effect, that there may be a problem with the continuing extradition agreement between Hong Kong and the United States. The Chinese government insisted on having a right of veto in case some Chinese person from Hong Kong was about to be extradited to the United States and was in possession of state secrets.

As such, it wasn't strictly speaking a bilateral agreement between Hong Kong and the United States because China would be looking over Hong Kong's shoulder. Still, China envisaged that this blocking mechanism would rarely, if ever, be applied and I frankly and honestly explained this to the American side. There was a rumble of disapproval and the enormous man eventually, after muttering with his team, said to me, 'Mr Hanratty you cannot be serious.' I realised that the game was up and there was no chance of implementing such an agreement. But I decided to score a point or two by saying I had no idea the American government's negotiating position borrowed language from Mr McEnroe's performance on

Centre Court at Wimbledon. We adjourned for an early lunch with no agreement in sight.

Another time, I flew to Moscow to negotiate a customs cooperation treaty with the Russian government. I had thought before I left that negotiations would be rough and tough and there would be a large amount of vodka consumed. I was right on the last point but wrong on the first. The Russian diplomat who led the Russian side was a delightful linguist with a subtle mind who, a week earlier, had negotiated with the French government in Paris and was now negotiating in fluent English with me.

During my time in Moscow I was hosted by a staunch supporter of the political regime. One day he took me on a sightseeing trip around Moscow and pointed to a statue of a man on a horse before asking me who it was. I replied, 'That is Marshall Zhukov who saved the world in the Great Patriotic War.' I deliberately used the Russian expression for World War II and was hugged by my host in response. After that I was given royal treatment for the rest of my trip.

Negotiations got off to a good start and towards the end of the week it seemed as though we might finish work on the treaty. I could see that the leader's face was falling as the prospect of a visit to Hong Kong diminished. So on the last day I announced that I felt the last two clauses were going to be rather difficult to negotiate. Therefore, we would have to finish them off in Hong Kong in six weeks' time. I looked forward to welcoming the Russian delegation there. There was great rejoicing and a splendid lunch with superb vodka. When the Russian delegation came out six weeks later we made a real fuss of them and took them to floating restaurants in Aberdeen and sightseeing trips. The negotiations were very successful indeed and the Russians returned home with a very favourable impression of the dynamism and efficiency of Hong Kong.

A common view was reached with the Chinese on a wide range of contracts and franchises due to straddle the handover, such as electricity, power, management of tunnels, bus and ferry services and container terminals and Air Service Agreements for scheduled flights in and out of Hong Kong. Experts from London came out to join our team. I found some of these negotiations technical and complex and sometimes struggled to master the detail but with copious use of midnight oil, I managed it.

My first serious task was the establishment of the Court of Final Appeal to replace appeals to the Judicial Committee of the Privy Council. I was well suited to this task as I had just been running the law courts in London and was familiar with the appeal system in Hong Kong. It was a significant achievement by the British and a generous gesture by the Chinese to allow the Court of Final Appeal to be established in Hong Kong and not Beijing.

As part of my briefing I flew back to London to see the Judicial Committee at work. The registrar was David Owen, a former colleague of mine in the Lord Chancellor's Department who was very helpful. One day I stepped out of my official car in Downing Street at the same time as Lord Lane, no longer the Lord Chief Justice but sitting on the Judicial Committee. We embraced each other like long lost brothers. I never saw the great man again.

The negotiations to establish the Court of Final Appeal turned out to be a minefield. The Joint Declaration provided that, 'Judges from other common law jurisdictions, as required, may be invited to sit on the Court of Final Appeal.' Many lawyers in Hong Kong had always assumed this meant the court would consist of five judges, three from Hong Kong and two leading judges from overseas. But the Chinese would not accept this. They insisted that the words 'as required' permitted the court to have no overseas judges some of the time. Moreover, the word 'judges' could be singular if interpreted as one from a panel of judges. So from two overseas judges there would occasionally be a panel from which the court would have no overseas judges at all and at the most just one. David and I had the unenviable task of trying to explain this to an incredulous Legislative Council of Hong Kong. We had a pretty rough ride. It was not our fault; we knew perfectly well that the

Chinese interpretation of the matter would hold sway because the Committee of the National People's Congress in Beijing, responsible for such interpretation, would always follow the Chinese line.

After an especially arduous day of fruitless negotiations we had a banquet with the Chinese side. Their ambassador rose and muttered a toast in Chinese. In Hong Kong the toast at banquets is 'yum sing', translated as 'bottoms up.' But the interpreter mangled the translation and said, 'Mr Ambassador he say, "Up your bottom."' It was one of those occasions when laughter from me was not called for; but this was made all the more difficult by one of our side who muttered rather too loudly, 'and up yours too.'

As we proceeded it became clear the Chinese side didn't want the Court of Final Appeal established before the handover in 1997. However, the British side wanted it up and running in advance of 1997 so the judges and officials could, as it were, get their eye in. Eventually, Governor Chris Patten decided that if the Chinese side continued to prevaricate he would introduce legislation in the Legislative Council of Hong Kong without the agreement of the Chinese side. This was called 'going unilateral.' He recognised it could have caused a serious row.

But I noticed that Michael Heseltine, then Secretary of State for Trade and Industry in the UK, was just about to lead a large delegation of British businessmen to China hoping to win contracts with Chinese companies up to the value of £1 billion. The visit was due to last about three weeks. Based on my wide Whitehall experience, I wrote a detailed memorandum to the top ten people in Hong Kong including the governor, outlining that Heseltine's visit would give an opportunity for us to have a further go at the Chinese in negotiations and to check over and over again the text of the legislation to ensure it was watertight. I made it clear we had three weeks to do this because there was no way the legislation could be put before the council unilaterally while Heseltine was doing his stuff in China. If we did put it before the council, the contracts would almost certainly be lost.

Once I had sent this memorandum, I received a phone call from a senior visiting diplomat from the British government who will remain nameless. He invited me to lunch and I was then taken to Va Bene, one of the top Italian restaurants in Hong Kong at that time. Here, over the minestrone soup, this gentleman asked whether I felt the British government could ever wish to implement a policy that would be contrary to the interests of the people of Hong Kong. I said of course they could; British history in Hong Kong did include much self-interest. This started with the East India Company polluting China with opium and receiving silver in return and, in more modern times, the Hong Kong Bank building being built from British steel rather than cheaper Korean steel. This did not go down well. To mitigate what I had said, I replied that of course the British government would always try to ensure its actions in Hong Kong favoured the best interests of Hong Kong people. But it may not always be practicable to follow such a clear line.

This diplomat then complained that my memorandum had caused a great deal of unhappiness among senior Hong Kong Chinese officials because it gave the impression that the British government would be willing to delay the legislation in order for Heseltine to secure his contracts. I said I expected just that to happen. The diplomat said I was entirely wrong. So I asked him to give me his word of honour that my memorandum was not based on fact and that the British government would not hesitate to go unilateral in the legislative council, even when Heseltine was in China. He gave me his word of honour and in return I questioned why he had taken me for such an expensive lunch. It concluded with Taylor's 1975 port. All he had to do, I said, was phone me and have a friendly chat. I told him I felt I was being 'got at' because, inadvertently, I had struck a raw nerve. I was unsure about the integrity of this diplomat's position. He insisted I was wrong and out of order.

In any event the legislation was indeed delayed until after Heseltine's visit to China. I forgot all about this as we eventually secured agreement with the Chinese side with the great help of the United States and the European Union. The US embassy in Beijing made it clear to the Chinese that the US government wished to have an independent and fair judicial system in Hong Kong after 1997, otherwise many of the American interests would pull out. So we achieved our legislation. I drafted the rules and we acquired the building near St John's Cathedral. The Court of Final Appeal would be up and running immediately after the handover with the much admired Chief Justice Andrew Li, in charge.

It was only on return to England and well after the handover that I read Jonathan Dimbleby's well researched and fascinating book *The Last Governor*. The book itself is all about the last years of the British administration in Hong Kong under Governor Chris Patten; a significant part of it focusses on the Court of Final Appeal's unilateral legislation and the Heseltine visit. It was revealed in that book that Malcolm Rifkind, the Foreign Secretary, had for the only time in his tenure ordered Chris Patten, his subordinate, not to introduce the legislation unilaterally in the Legislative Council until after Mr Heseltine had got his contracts. I had been right all along; I was very disappointed.

I could well imagine what had happened, how this diplomat, who was well oiled with that port, must have returned to his colleagues and observed that, 'After a good lunch Hanratty is anyone's.' It didn't show much respect for me. What he should have done was to tell me that my memorandum had caused a good deal of anxiety because I was entirely right and that I should not do it again without consultation. Instead, he had chosen to take me to an expensive lunch and lie through his teeth. I was aggrieved to have been treated so cynically by a diplomat I had previously admired. Still, perhaps he was just following orders; it isn't easy being a diplomat and matters are rarely black and white, just different shades of grey. My feelings mattered little in the wide scheme of things.

Years later, Sir Malcolm Rifkind was the speaker at a dinner I was chairing at the Athenaeum. We discussed this incident and he remembered the row well. I was impressed by his courtesy and charm, as well as his wide diplomatic and political knowledge. He was a brilliant, wise and elegant Foreign Secretary, sadly set up by journalists later over financial inducements. He deserved better after his long public service. More recently, I spoke to Jonathan Dimbleby and he remembered the row well too.

During that time in Hong Kong we also had to 'localise' much of the existing law that had simply been transferred from the UK to Hong Kong. This involved amending legislation on numerous topics before it was passed through the Legislative Council in order to become Hong Kong law.

More disputes arose surrounding Defence Lands. All over Hong Kong there were about thirty sites occupied by the British garrison, soldiers, sailors and airmen. There was a large hospital, an airfield and the prize of all, the Prince of Wales Barracks, in the central area of Hong Kong, which resembled a large inverted gin bottle. These properties were owned by the Hong Kong government and assigned to the British garrison for defence purposes. If the garrison didn't need any of the estate it had to hand it back to the Hong Kong government.

The dilemma was that the Hong Kong government wanted to sell gradually discarded defence estates on the open market for vast profits, but the Chinese government said it wanted all the defence estates for itself. The negotiations were extremely tough and talks went on for months with some pretty undignified horse trading. Eventually an agreement was reached. Although the Chinese acquired the Prince of Wales building, the basin next to it was filled in. A separate harbour was built for Chinese warships away from the central area on Stonecutters Island. Both sides were content.

Another tricky task, which took me five years to complete, was redrafting the boundary of Hong Kong. This had initially been settled by the Lockhart Wong Agreement of 1899 and consisted of an agreement on the land and the sea boundary. The sea boundary, in particular, was very odd as it cut through the end of Lantau Island and did not allow sufficient space around two smaller islands to the south of Hong Kong, in particular an island called Po Toi. It was an interesting exercise. Over those five years I tramped across the whole border of Hong Kong; I climbed hills where the old stones had been laid; and I was taken by the Royal Marines in a rib at forty knots in Deep Bay. One day I was flown by helicopter with a few others to the border post run by the Royal Hong Kong Police Dog Unit. I was briefed and given a splendid lunch. I thanked the hosts in my speech for serving sizzling beef Sichuan style. They giggled. I then realised it was a sizzling Alsatian I had been eating.

In the course of the work we took the opportunity of tidying up the boundary where it wasn't clear. My naval experience proved very useful because British Admiralty charts had been used to form the sea boundary. A recognised international measurement was used throughout that part of the world, WGS84, except in Hong Kong. The consequence was that a latitude and longitude precise position could be as much as 200 metres apart using different measurements. I agreed to use the internationally recognised one, which helped secure the sea boundary in order that there was no potential confusion. The boundary was extended to one nautical mile off islands such as Po Toi and round the end of Lantau. We called these 'bubbles' in our negotiations.

Eventually, after five years, we signed a memorandum of understanding (MOU) recognising the new territorial boundaries. John Ashton, later the climate change adviser to the FCO, tidied up my draft of the MOU. He was a supremely fit walker over the hilly Hong Kong terrain and we worked happily and successfully together. To celebrate the achievement of the MOU, I chartered a Hong Kong Marine Police launch and took the Chinese and the British sides out to a wonderful restaurant in Po Toi where we devoured the most delicious crabs and prawns. I had brought decent champagne with me and filled the glasses before announcing there would be a toast. The Chinese became very serious thinking that I was going to make a toast to the Chinese leadership or whatever. Much to their surprise, I simply held the bubbling champagne glass up and said the toast was to 'bubbles'. The laughter went on for about five minutes. I got on singularly well with the Chinese side and recognised that they were under a lot of pressure individually. This explained why they were so cautious. But in my view they were always honest and trustworthy. Their lawyers in particular were internationally educated at mainly American universities and were highly competent.

As 1997 approached, the handover of Hong Kong to China became ever more important in political terms in the UK. So after David Edwards left in 1995 and I took over, I was closely watched and advised by Sir Franklin Berman, the distinguished Foreign Office legal advisor, and Sherard Cowper-Coles, the head of the Hong Kong Department. Sherard subsequently became the ambassador to Israel, then to Saudi Arabia and finally to Afghanistan. He was knighted and was a brave and resourceful diplomat and a great support, adviser and guide to me.

One of the major rows leading up to the handover stemmed from the wish of Governor Patten to make the election system to the Legislative Council more obviously democratic with fewer appointed places. This was outside my field but I watched the proceedings carefully because if there was a row with the Chinese side then my negotiations the next day would go nowhere.

I came to admire Governor Chris Patten for his courage and determination in wanting to improve the democratic process, though he may not have fully realised the Chinese had waited 140 years to regain Hong Kong and were perfectly capable of waiting another eighteen months to ensure that Beijing supporters were in the majority. Still, one of the governor's most impressive achievements was that he gave the people of Hong Kong the confidence to realise they not only had obligations to a government but also rights from a government. They were able to demonstrate. If there was a sign of self-censorship in the press it would be spotted.

When Patten visited Hong Kong a few years after the handover as a European commissioner and gave a press conference, he was given a standing ovation by the local Chinese press. During the handover he benefitted from the wise advice of Edward Llewellyn, his special adviser, now chief of staff at 10 Downing Street. I was fascinated by how much sheer intellectual and linguistic firepower was available to us in Hong Kong from the FCO and elsewhere and how young many of these brilliant advisers were.

My job also had a public presentation role too. The Japanese would take me and a colleague out to an excellent Japanese restaurant every six weeks to ask how the negotiations were going. We invariably presented an optimistic picture even though we may have had one or two problems. But then, of course, the Japanese, being resourceful, would take the Chinese side out too and sometimes they received a rather different view. I soon put a stop to this by ensuring over friendly drinks with the Chinese that we all spoke from the same hymn sheet for the purposes of confidence in Hong Kong.

I also had some amusing moments. In the course of numerous meetings to decide which treaties could remain in force after the handover, we discussed arbitration. Our bottom line was that the New York Convention on the Enforcement of Arbitral Awards must remain but two older Geneva Conventions could be discarded. I let the Chinese side speak first and they came out with precisely this proposal. I then said the British side needed to consider the Chinese side's proposals and therefore we needed half an hour's adjournment.

My team was aghast and reminded me forcibly that the Chinese side's proposals were precisely ours too. I told them to concentrate on eating the sticky buns, which always seemed to be provided, and count to 500 slowly. Then we re-joined the Chinese side. I said something like, 'The British side having very carefully considered the Chinese side's proposals, and after much discussion, would like to praise the Chinese side for their recognition of the importance of the New York Convention and its application in the common law and statute law of Hong Kong. The Chinese side's proposals will not only be a great help to Hong Kong after the handover but also to China too.'

I carried on like this for about ten minutes flattering the other side, giving them all the credit and accepting their proposals before doing the deal. There was no point scoring. In this way I was able to make real progress on difficult matters with the Chinese side because I never sought to try to win an argument by shallow debating points. This kind of behaviour would have annoyed the other side and delayed any agreement.

On another occasion there was a row with the Chinese side over Vietnamese boat people. The Chinese at the JLG blamed the British for allowing the Vietnamese in. Eventually a deal was done at international level in Geneva; Vietnam would receive boat people who were returning economic migrants without taking punitive action. There was a clear distinction made between those who were refugees and those who were economic migrants; this is ironic in view of the mass immigration to Europe. There was a problem in that the Vietnamese refused to take back even economic migrant boat people who were of Chinese ethnic origin. The refusal was unlawful but the British and Hong Kong authorities could do little about it. There were unfortunate television news items showing struggling Vietnamese migrants being forced up the steps into aircraft in order to be removed. They were petrified of being repatriated as they feared ill treatment on return. But international monitors were in place in Vietnam to check on the welfare of those returned. This worked well.

The Hong Kong method of handling the Vietnamese boat people was a public relations disaster. Children and mothers were held behind barbed wire in camps which looked like prisons. They had committed no crime but simply wished to leave Vietnam at great risk to themselves. It was a sad example of man's inhumanity to man which unfortunately persists in relation to migrants today. There were certain similarities with those boat people and the migrants of today. Some were genuine and frightened. Others were just seeking a better life and wanted eventual settlement in the USA. These kinds of dilemmas were to haunt me when I became an immigration judge.

In order to persuade Vietnamese migrants to leave Hong Kong and return to Vietnam, life in the camps was deliberately made less attractive. Initially, kindly and concerned professional expatriate women, including my wife Pam, sponsored by a Dutch charity, were allowed into the camps to help the women and men earn a few dollars. The Vietnamese created attractive needlepoint tapestries such as table napkins and cushion covers. However, the helpers, including Pam, were soon refused entry to the camps as it was thought that they were making life more attractive to the Vietnamese in those camps, which may cause a reluctance for them to leave.

Another problem at this time arose over which law would apply to the Chinese People's Liberation Army garrisoned in Hong Kong. The local Hong Kong people were only too well aware that the PLA had shot and killed its own people on 4 June 1989 in Tiananmen Square. They also knew that in China the PLA was, in practice, above the law. If a PLA lorry ran over a pedestrian in China the civilian police would not interfere. What would happen in Hong Kong?

The position was complicated by the indolence of the Hong Kong government and its Attorney General's Chambers in particular. If a British Army lorry ran over a pedestrian in central Hong Kong, the British garrison would pay compensation providing the lorry driver was clearly at fault. But if there was uncertainty on liability and the garrison refused to pay, the only remedy was to bring a civil action for damages in London. The Hong Kong Crown Proceedings Ordinance didn't allow the garrison to be sued in Hong Kong. That ordinance should have been amended years previously. The Chinese side had done their research and the many embarrassing privileges of the garrison which lay rotting on the statute book of Hong Kong were exposed to modern and embarrassing light.

The PLA team with whom we negotiated were bright and resourceful. They were international businessmen rather than soldiers and did not go in for drunken rice wine toasts at dinner. Rather they preferred serious working lunches. Eventually, the garrison law was unveiled in Beijing. It was not too bad. The PLA to its credit had listened carefully. If a soldier committed a wrong in Hong Kong and was on duty, the action would have to be brought in Beijing courts. On the other hand, criminal offences would be dealt with in service courts. Off duty offences would come before local civilian courts in Hong Kong. There was some ambivalence about the meaning of the words 'on duty' but the problem was resolved, partly because the Chinese garrison in Hong Kong behaved impeccably after the handover.

When I visited Hong Kong on several occasions in subsequent years I would see well behaved Chinese soldiers bird watching in the New Territories with expensive cameras. It was perhaps revealing that I did not see any locals talking with them. The relationship was distant.

Meanwhile the JLG continued its work, discussing the assets of Hong Kong, the archives, the handover ceremonies, defence and public order, intellectual property and numerous international treaties. Sometimes the negotiations were difficult, at others progress was swift.

In early 1997 a senior Chinese official approached me and in fluent English said that the Chinese government would be pleased if I stayed on after the handover. I was at my most pompous and replied, 'I am very flattered by this offer. Is it because of my perceived negotiating skills, or knowledge of the law or respect for

Chinese history and culture?' 'Oh no,' he replied. 'It is because you cooperate!' I asked him not to mention this to Mr Patten and remarked that it was really the turn of the Chinese to run Hong Kong so I would return to London. The kind offer was not repeated.

Throughout that time I was giving private interviews to lawyers and politicians from all over the world who wanted to be briefed about the state of the negotiations. Obviously, I couldn't breach any official secrets but I could bring some sense of order to the ideas people had. I regularly gave lectures to top solicitors' firms in Hong Kong and they were always very generous, offering to pay a large fee. Naturally I couldn't accept such a fee but I would indicate that some wine would go down rather well. Subsequently a case of fine claret would wing its way to the Attorney General's Chambers, where it was declared and shared out among my colleagues.

On the subject of wine, there was one rather embarrassing moment from that time that still stands out. A visiting senior judge from England arrived with his wife, a former colleague in the Lord Chancellor's Department at undersecretary level, both of whom very influential. I received permission from the Attorney General's Chambers to take them to lunch at an excellent Chinese restaurant. I invited, among others, a representative from the Army, the Solicitor General, a judge and a business person so that a good mixture of us sat down for this splendid Chinese meal. There were English, Australian and Chinese present.

A waiter in a morning coat came in pushing a trolley on which bottles of wine were displayed. I asked him whether these were house wines and he said they were. So, without looking at the labels, I ordered three red and three white bottles. When the red had been poured the judge from England, who was a master of wine, spun the drink in his glass expertly, gazed at it and said, 'James you continue to surprise me. I did not realise you were a wine expert. This is a Margaux Grand Cru.' Panic! I asked the waiter to show me the bottles and how much each cost. Each bottle came in at £120. I had ordered six.

After the meal I went back to the Attorney General's Chambers to see the finance officer, Peter Chan, who was always highly competent, numerate and amusing. I told the whole story to him and said that I didn't expect the Hong Kong government to pay all of this bill but I would pay £500 for my own incompetence and the government could pay the rest. Peter was quite wonderful and said that owing to my honesty the Hong Kong government would pay the lot; and it did.

Not long after this my friend Clinton Leeks, the former private secretary to the governor, introduced me to the directors of a leading Austrian bank and asked me to give them a presentation. As a consequence, a month later, I received an invitation to go to Vienna to give the formal annual lecture on behalf of this bank. I would be addressing 400 top business people and diplomats on the subject of Hong Kong. The two previous speakers, I learned, had been Helmut Schmidt, the former German Chancellor and Henry Kissinger.

I realised that as soon as the invitation became public within the Hong Kong government and the Foreign Office I would be discarded and someone far more important would be sent in my place. Naughtily I kept the invitation quiet while I wrote a very careful speech lasting forty minutes for them. I also asked a representative of the Austrian bank to translate the first two pages into phonetic German so that I, a non-German speaker, could at least recite the introductory paragraphs in German. The audience expected the talk to be given in English.

Three weeks before I was due to leave, I made the invitation known. There was nothing anybody could do about it except, of course, clear the speech both in London and in Hong Kong. I flew out to Vienna and deliberately paid a call on Sir Anthony Figgis, the British Ambassador to Austria, because he was entitled to know what was going on in his patch. He was very welcoming and gave me a useful brief on Austrian politics. A few years later I played tennis for the Hurlingham Club against the Diplomatic Corps; by chance, Sir Anthony was their captain.

On the day of the speech I was escorted down a large centre aisle and was introduced. Behind a lectern I gave my talk on the history of Hong Kong and what was going on there at the present time, paying particular attention to the negotiations and the important financial consequences for all involved. I made some jokes but not many. It went down very well indeed. Afterwards, I was invited to other events during my week's stay. I spoke extensively and, as it were, became a missionary on behalf of Hong Kong.

There was one awkward incident which occurred as I was being shown around Vienna and I spotted an unusual memorial. It had a column with skeletal human figures around the outside of it. I asked what this was and was told by my guide that it was a memorial to Jewish people who had 'died' at a camp nearby during the war. I do not think she was anti-Semitic but just a little too casual in acknowledging the terrible deeds done under the Third Reich. I asked her to stop the car. I got out and walked up to this monument. I stood to attention, bowed and returned to the car; point made.

I considered leaving the legal adviser position I held when I found out the Hong Kong government and the judiciary wanted a new chief executive to run the court service. In typical Hong Kong style a team travelled to Australia, New Zealand and the UK looking for the ideal person. They had 287 applications and interviewed eighty candidates. The salary was enormous. I felt I could make a contribution so I applied; I was interviewed by a panel of no less than eight, including the sparkling Mrs Anson Chan, the chief secretary of the Hong Kong civil service. I was unsuccessful, though later I learned that the judges wanted me but the civil service people were keen to appoint a senior female Chinese-speaking civil servant. I have to concede they were right. I was second. The job had to go to a competent Chinese speaker and this lady did very well.

We all had a very good social life in Hong Kong in both an official and unofficial capacity. Official parties included celebrating important national days of various countries such as St. Patrick's Day. For the St Patrick's Day Ball there were 400 present with 300 on the waiting list. Groups of Irish musicians and dancers would fly out from Dublin. These parties were lavish, well organised and fun. There were also parties at the Hong Kong Club, the Royal Hong Kong Yacht Club and with colleagues. We went sailing often and had rallies with other boats.

I had my fiftieth birthday party in 1996 at the Royal Hong Kong Yacht Club, where I remain a Life Member. One day I was walking to the Star Ferry when I spotted some South American buskers by the underpass. They played beautifully on pipes in a way that reminded me of the music in the film *The Mission*. I approached them and said, 'Are you are going to be the music at my party?' One of them replied in fluent English that I had better go and see their agent first. I was astonished. I told them I thought they were just buskers, not an organisation with an agent. Nevertheless, I paid an exorbitant fee and they agreed to perform. Halfway through the dinner they all marched in wearing their South American dress, taking nearly everyone by surprise. They played beautifully.

My friend John Hunter, a brilliant Australian lawyer and a fine opening batsman for our cricket team the Legal Eagles, stood up and delivered his toast. 'Hanratty comes from the Lord Chancellor's Department in the House of Lords,' he said. There were cries of 'Oooh'. He continued, 'I have been to the Lord Chancellor's Department but, of course, being an Australian I had to go in by the back door. Do you know, ladies and gentlemen, in the Lord Chancellor's Department they wear black jackets and pin-striped trousers and have an exaggerated sense of their own self-importance. Well, ladies and gentlemen, I have good news for you. Since Hanratty came to Hong Kong he has dispensed with the black jacket and pin-striped trousers but not, of course, the exaggerated sense of self-importance.' There was a huge roar from the guests. I recognised it wasn't just John's sense of humour they were laughing at; there must have been an element of truth in it.

I also occasionally used to do the readings at the Catholic Cathedral in Hong Kong in front of about 1,000 people. Chris Patten used to attend, sitting in his reserved place with his family in the front row. Sometimes I was rather naughty. I would recite the bidding prayers, praying for world peace or for the victims of some typhoon but occasionally I would invent bidding prayers unofficially such as, 'Lord, may Human Rights continue to be applied in Hong Kong after the handover. Lord hear us.' In English and Cantonese 1,000 people would utter, 'Lord graciously hear us.' I would glance down to see the governor sitting in the front row sucking his spectacles. The look on his face clearly said, 'James, if you do that again you will be in trouble.' He never missed much. I always admired his courage, integrity and intellect.

Early on in my time in Hong Kong I was invited to join the Thursday Club, a lunch society at The Hong Kong Club, presided over by Gilbert Rodway, QC. The members were distinguished bankers, lawyers and judges; I believe I was invited not for any special characteristics that I had to offer but because they hoped to find out what was going on with the negotiations with the Chinese. I was always very careful not to breach any official secrets. They were very sociable occasions and some of the members had titles which greatly appealed to Gilbert. We would usually invite a guest each time, somebody like Sir David Tang who did much to smooth relations with China and the Commander British Forces General Sir John Foley. We could find out from their point of view what was going on and in a very convivial atmosphere. I greatly cherished these lunches.

More frivolously, I was asked to join another lunch club called The Boys. The lunches were also held at The Hong Kong Club on the first Friday of each month. In order to be admitted, I had to write an essay explaining why they should not actually accept me. I wrote that, having failed to play cricket for Yorkshire I was sent to school in Lancashire. I subsequently advised the Lord Chancellor on Rhodesia but it changed its name, on the European Bankruptcy Convention which we never joined and on a Human Rights Commission which we never had. When I advised the Lord Chancellor on judicial appointments I expected all candidates male or female to behave like gentlemen. On return to Hong Kong I experienced success, for which I should rightfully be revered, like visa abolition with San Marino and the transfer of latrines at Osborne Barracks to the PLA. In my spare time I sailed and raced yachts like Captain Pugwash assisted by Seaman Staines. I said I had a long suffering wife who for some reason all my friends considered a saint. The result was successful as I was elected for the next Friday lunch! The club itself was presided over by Peter Graham, a sophisticated and amusing New Zealand lawyer. We had great fun and even adjourned occasionally to have lunch in Macau.

During that time we had a number of wonderful holidays as a family, including three weeks visiting the islands of Hawaii which was the best of them all. Memories remain of music, sunsets and beaches.

Richard was settled at Stonyhurst College while Alexandra enjoyed and worked exceptionally well at St Mary's, Ascot. Pam often had to return to England to look after her widowed mother who was very demanding. On those occasions I would be left with Susie, aged about seven, and our maid Conny. I used to enjoy going to Bentleys, an oyster and fish bar modelled on the one in England. It served delicious fish pie, incorporating grapes. I became very friendly with the Chinese waiting staff and one day I telephoned and asked them to reserve a discreet table for two because I wished to bring my girlfriend along. Fortunately, I said, my wife was in England. I also asked whether they could make a cake inscribed 'To Daddy with Love.' I explained that this girlfriend of mine called me Daddy. The staff were very concerned and wondered whether I should be doing this. I told them to make sure the table was ready.

That day I asked Conny to clothe Susie in her best evening dress and she put a tiara on her blonde head. We went down to Bentleys. I walked in first, attracted the attention of all the staff, found my discreet table and then produced my 'girlfriend', a glamorous grinning Susie. The staff relaxed with laughter and relief. The cake to Daddy was of course intended for my birthday. The staff were so delighted that they refused to charge me for this delicious cake. It was all such fun.

12

THE HANDOVER

Meanwhile, the plans for the farewell to Hong Kong on 30 June 1997 were in full swing. The British decided to conduct a farewell a few hours before midnight so the Chinese authorities wouldn't have to be consulted about it. This was going to be an open air parade at HMS *Tamar* with stands around the tennis courts and music to be played by the Hong Kong Philharmonic Orchestra. Prince Charles, based in the Royal Yacht Britannia, would preside. Beforehand we had a meeting about this organised by the head of the British side of the JLG, Hugh Davies.

I indicated at this meeting attended by about twenty other people that I wished to ask a non-legal question. Hugh, ever patient, said I was always doing this but please proceed. I asked what would happen if it rained. He turned to Mr Wong of the Royal Observatory who told him there was only a ten per cent chance of precipitation. I said that if it did rain, it would be like monsoon stair-rods. We would all get drenched. Hugh turned to Mr Wong again who said, 'We have a contingency plan. That is, we have ten thousand umbrellas which we can issue to all the guests watching this parade.' I indicated that I thought this was a cue for laughter but it turned out to be deadly serious. After that I kept quiet.

After attending an auction at HMS *Tamar* to buy certain artefacts from the mess, the British farewell proceeded. There was a magnificent parade where sailors in tropical kit marched into the arena led by a splendid Royal Navy officer about six-foot-six in height with a ramrod back carrying his sword. And then the heavens opened; it poured. We all got soaked except the orchestra. There was only one covered stand and that was for the Hong Kong

Philharmonic Orchestra who played Elgar's *Nimrod* so movingly. Everyone, except the orchestra, including the governor and Prince Charles was drenched.

Nevertheless, the parade was emotional. We all put our umbrellas up. I was in the VIP stand and the water from my umbrella dripped down the back of Stanley Ho, the Macau casino magnate. But we all tried to appear as though we didn't mind. It was extraordinary that the British and Hong Kong authorities did not cover the stands to keep people dry.

After this ceremony we all trooped into the Convention Centre, which had been newly completed, for a dinner. There were 2,000 people there, including the Chinese side. As we walked in another problem became apparent: the air condition was so fierce it put everyone who was wet at risk of pneumonia. Fortunately, I was going to the farewell party at the Royal Hong Kong Yacht Club afterwards and had a bag with me containing some spare and less formal clothes.

I went into the Convention Centre and saw a sign saying 'Changing Room C'. I dived in there and was standing in the corner with my trousers around my ankles when suddenly, the door burst open. There stood the clerk to the new Chief Justice, Andrew Li. This clerk abruptly said the room was reserved for the Chief Justice. I replied, with an astonished Andrew listening behind him that I was sure the Chief Justice would not wish me to spoil this great occasion by walking into the Convention Centre in my underpants even if they were by Calvin Klein. So I changed into dry clothes and was about the only person there apart from the Chinese side who was comfortable. But we did have a splendid banquet despite the speeches lasting rather too long.

We left just before midnight for the actual handover ceremony. There were two flagpoles, one for the Chinese flag and the other with the Union Jack. There was a Chinese guard of honour with fixed bayonets and a very fine Chinese military band which I thought rather outshone the band from the Brigade of Guards.

(Right) My grandfather Andrew Belton and his bride Marie Babin on their wedding day
© Corbis

(Below) With my parents, aged three months

(Above) At prep school aged 10 (far right)

(Lower Left) Playing cricket aged 11

(Lower Right) With my wife Pam at a wedding in 1975

(Right) My three children Richard, Susie and Alexandra at the Hurlingham Club, 2011

(Middle) With Pam, Alexandra and Susie in Positano, Italy, 2013

(Bottom) The Hanratty family celebrating my father's 90th birthday in 2009

(Above) The minesweeper HMS *Glasserton*, Bay of Biscay, 1980. I'm manning the bridge

(Right) My pride and joy *Alana III*. Sailing with Tom Cunliffe and friends, Solent, 2011

(Below) Wearing the white ensign on board *Alana III* during a Royal Yacht Squadron rally, 2014

(Left) Pam in Italy, 2005

(Below) With Pam at the Royal Yacht Squadron's Bicentenary Ball, 2015

(Above) Stonyhurst College, Lancashire, from the air
Credit: Stonyhurst College

(Below) The Royal Yacht Squadron, Cowes, from the air
Credit: Rolex

(Left) The Athenaeum Club on Pall Mall
Credit: The Athenaeum

(Middle) The Hurlingham Club in Fulham
© The Hurlingham Club

(Bottom) The Royal Courts of Justice on the Strand
© Gregobagel/iStock

(Above) Refugees arrive on the shores of Lesbos, Greece, in an inflatable boat, February 2016
Credit: ARIS MESSINIS/AFP/Getty Images

(Below) A railway line to nowhere: migrant camp on the Greek-Macedonian border, March 2016
Credit: SAKIS MITROLDIS/AFP/Getty Images

Then there were speeches. Chris Patten gave a deeply thoughtful, generous and kind speech in which he indicated that the British were passing the baton to the Chinese government in accordance with the agreements made and wished both Hong Kong and China well. As was usual with Chris Patten, this speech was masterly.

The Chinese side were senior unsmiling politicians from Beijing, the so called 'waxwork' figures as described by HRH Prince Charles, whose perceptive words were unhappily leaked. Their main speaker was disappointingly ungracious and merely said they were looking forward to their right to resume the sovereignty of Hong Kong. There was no mention, for example, that although the Chinese had never recognised the British right to be in Hong Kong, the Chinese government nevertheless was appreciative of the thriving and successful city created by the British with local Chinese input which was now being handed over. I suppose for reasons of face or otherwise it was not possible for a Chinese speaker to be so generous.

However, this did leave a slightly disappointing feeling. I had hoped his speech would display mutual respect and regard. Shortly after this, one flag was lowered and the other went up which triggered the Chinese to clap vigorously. I looked at the senior British officials who were sitting there. Most were ashen-faced wondering what on earth they had done.

I left the Convention Centre and went down to a thriving party at the Royal Hong Kong Yacht Club just in time to see HMS *Chatham* and the Royal Yacht Britannia steaming past on their way out to the South China Sea. It was deeply emotional. People were in tears, but also there was an air of excitement about it all. The next day under Chinese sovereignty I went to a whole string of parties at places like the Mandarin Oriental Hotel in Hong Kong with people from all over the world who had come to see the new Hong Kong Special Administrative Region of China. Some expected Chinese soldiers to be everywhere, but there were none to be seen. The Chinese garrison stayed only a matter of days, leaving just a few well behaved soldiers behind who remained in their barracks most of the time.

I am pleased to observe that at least up to a few months ago China has abided by the terms of the Joint Declaration and has acted very honourably towards Hong Kong. But the disturbing development towards the end of 2015 when five publishers and booksellers who specialised in detailed stories of the Chinese elite were abducted from Hong Kong and spirited away to China is most disturbing. Our Foreign Secretary raised the matter on a visit to Beijing and was curtly told to mind his own business as this was 'an internal matter for China'. It was no such thing; the Sino-British Joint Declaration of 1984, a treaty between China and the UK government stipulated at paragraph 151 that 'Freedom of the person, of speech [and] of the press' shall be maintained. No doubt our diplomats reminded our Foreign Secretary to mention this treaty obligation to his Chinese opposite number or perhaps they forgot to do so for wider diplomatic reasons!

I still maintain that the handover was the greatest British diplomatic triumph since World War II, a lasting legacy of those brilliant men and women who engineered it all. We left Hong Kong as a family, holidayed in Malaysia for two weeks and then returned to our house in Putney to start our life in England all over again. It was with sadness and reluctance that we flew off and out of the place that we loved and still do.

There was one footnote to our time in Hong Kong; in 2009 Pam and I returned to Hong Kong with Susie for a holiday. As we flew in, Pam and I were behaving like interested tourists. However, Susie became very emotional. She felt she was returning home. It was very interesting to see her excitement and enthusiasm.

One afternoon I decided on the spur of the moment to go to see the Court of Final Appeal which I had established. I was wearing a blazer and tie and looking reasonably smart. I walked in and said to a clerk that, as a junior judge in England, I would very much like to pay a respectful courtesy call on the Chief Justice Andrew Li. Just imagine doing this in England. I would have been despatched from the Royal Courts of Justice rather smartly and told to write to request an appointment. But in Hong Kong, I was simply asked to wait.

After twenty minutes a well-dressed clerk approached me and said he understood I was a judge in England and wished to see the Chief Justice. I said I would very much like to call upon him again as I had a part in the establishment of the Court of Final Appeal. It would only be a courtesy call of about five minutes or so, if he was free. The clerk disappeared. He then returned and asked if I could prove I was a judge. I replied that I was there on holiday but then I had a brainwave. I said, 'If you have got a copy of *Who's Who*, I am in it.' Twenty minutes later a pristine copy of the book arrived in the hands of this clerk with the page opened at my entry. I pointed to it and said, 'That is me.' However, he then said to me, 'Can you prove that this is you?' I was surprised. Fortunately, and with great triumph, I was able to produce my newly acquired Royal Hong Kong Yacht Club membership card which included a photograph. The clerk then disappeared with my card and the copy of *Who's Who*. Twenty minutes later he appeared again, returned the card and said that the Chief Justice would see me now.

I was shown into the quarters of Andrew Li, who was a renowned figure in Hong Kong for his intellect. He was widely admired for the way he had steered the judiciary through the minefield of the Hong Kong Special Administrative Region of China while preserving the common law system and the independence of the judiciary. As the clerk showed me in I saw that I was being given the tea ceremony. A splendid tea was laid out with beautiful Chinese porcelain. We sat down and talked about the Court of Final Appeal and the work that it was doing, including that with the help of foreign judges, one at a time.

Afterwards he showed me round, taking me to the court rooms and the offices. He stayed with me for about an hour.

Finally, he escorted me to the front door to say goodbye. I knew from my previous experience in Hong Kong that this was not a way of pushing me out of the building as it may be thought in English terms but was a sign of respect in that he had escorted me to the door. I was greatly and deeply touched by this little kindness. When I returned to England and wrote him a formal letter of thanks I remarked on this singular honour he had shown to me. I know that he was pleased that I had noticed. I then took the opportunity of inviting him to address the Hong Kong Society in England, where I was on the committee, at our annual dinner at the Grosvenor House Hotel. He did attend and gave a most interesting and thoughtful speech about the work of the judiciary and the application of the law in Hong Kong. I was seated next to him during that evening. The honour was mine.

13

SAILING

For many decades now sailing has been a passion of mine. It is a particularly rewarding pursuit because so many different qualities are required to be successful. The skipper has to meet the challenge. He or she must be competent, safety-conscious, capable of inspiring confidence in the crew, a good navigator, and a leader always mindful of the interests of individual members. It is a very good test of leadership which I learned from my experience in the RNR.

When I went to Hong Kong in 1991 I bought a Yamaha 30, a Japanese yacht thirty-feet-long. Unfortunately, she was called *Maiko* which means 'trainee Geisha girl' in Japanese. This did not find favour with my wife. So I decided to change the name to *Alana* after my two daughters, Alexandra and Susannah. But I had not reckoned with the superstition of Chinese boat people. I was told that, as I had changed the name, no Chinese electrician or engineer or mechanic would come on board my boat until a proper name changing ceremony had occurred; the boat was jinxed. The devils would run all over it; the boat was 'bad joss.'

Accordingly, I had to dress this boat overall, which means putting the flags up the mast fore and aft, in Peng Chau Island where there was a Chinese temple. Here we worshipped on our knees, burnt paper money offerings and left real money as a present. We took all this very seriously out of respect for the temple and its priests. We were presented with a cooked side of a pig, which appeared burned but was later found to be delicious. We turned the boat three times in front of the temple, sounding the horn each time we passed. The fishermen then all blew their sirens on their fishing boats as we were blessed and absolved from our sins. There was no more difficulty with local Chinese workers on the boat.

When I mentioned this event casually to my mother, a devout Catholic, she was appalled that I had worshipped at a pagan shrine. So I wheeled out a Jesuit priest, Father John Russell, who was the padre for Hong Kong University and took him out on the boat. He sprayed it with holy water and blessed it. After that I was doubly protected. The boat served us well; on one occasion we came third in a race to Macau out of forty boats because I had calculated the tides more accurately than others. The other yachts found themselves beating into a Force 5 wind but I was way up north and swept down on a broad reach passing nearly all of them with whoops of triumph.

At this time Pam's mother became ill so Pam had to return to the UK to be with her for long periods. Richard and Alexandra were at Stonyhurst and St Mary's Ascot respectively, so I used to sail in *Alana* often just with Susie. She became a fine instinctive sailor. One weekend we sailed thirty miles to Shelter Cove, an outstation of the Royal Hong Kong Yacht Club. We went alongside *Marinero*, a sleek Swan 47 belonging to marine lawyer Mike Stevens, a good friend. As Susie passed from one boat to another a shoe fell off into the South China Sea. One of Mike's crew dubbed Susie, the 'Shoeless One'. The name stuck for years at the RHKYC. Susie was always irritated that she hadn't been born aged fifteen. She watched with a mixture of longing and amazement at the party on board *Marinero* with all these good looking, intelligent, single male and female lawyers and bankers dancing away, revelling in each other's scintillating company.

Just before the handover of Hong Kong to China in 1997 I took part in a race to the Philippines called the South China Sea Race in a larger yacht owned by Professor John Sanderson and his wife Dr Julia Billingham, which I navigated. It was great fun. The Sandersons were good sailors, who subsequently sailed around the world together. The race was just over 500 miles and took three days; we were escorted by a Royal Navy patrol craft to whom we reported twice a day for safety purposes. Alexandra came too and distinguished herself by repairing a hole in the mainsail with a huge needle and thread. The job was well done and took hours.

During the race there were two twelve-hour holes with no wind. Yet somehow one of the yachts skippered by a Hong Kong businessman made fifty miles of progress down the track when everyone else was becalmed; obviously he had been using his engine. Inevitably, this gentleman won a prize. It was extraordinary that in the Royal Hong Kong Yacht Club, with 300 people mingling together, his prize was presented in total silence.

On return to the UK after the handover I joined the RNVR Yacht Club; an organisation for RNR and RN officers and other good sailors. I joined the committee and eventually was made a rear commodore in charge of the club boat, *Volunteer*, where I would have to examine potential skippers to make sure they were competent to take the boat out. Needless to say, the one who nearly ran aground on the Bramble Bank was not found to be competent!

In due course I became the commodore of this club for two years which involved a considerable amount of work organising rallies and social events including an annual dinner. We were fortunate to have as our admiral His Royal Highness Prince Michael of Kent who joined us for one of our dinners. I had three of these dinners, one at the Naval Club in Hill Street in London and the other two at the Athenaeum and the Hurlingham Club. The First Sea Lord, Sir Alan (later Lord) West, was the guest of honour at one such dinner and Rear Admiral Sir Jeremy de Halpert at another. I was very grateful to them. I was succeeded by Commander Tom Cunningham, RD, RNR, a distinguished civil engineer and a good friend.

Meanwhile, I had become an RYA Yachtmaster after completing the required mileage, a week's course and a demanding practical exam. Indeed, our tutor for the course was a tough sailor with a ring in his ear who announced confidently after the first day of teaching that none of us would pass because we were all absolutely hopeless. I nearly walked off the boat with an American but we stuck it out and by the end of the course we worshipped this guy because he had converted us into an efficient fighting crew. We all passed the exam.

In 2003 the RNVR Yacht Club sailed to St Valery en Caux in northern France for a rally. Here the 51st Highland Division had fought a brave rear guard action before Dunkirk. We went there to lay a wreath at the cemetery with French officials. We all lined up in three ranks. Nigel Hayler, a brave and skilled former Fleet Air Arm pilot, whose godmother, incidentally, was Pam's aunt, was guard commander. He ordered us all to button up our blazers. There were at least three sounds of buttons popping. Then he gave the immortal command, 'Gentlemen of The Yacht Club, off caps.' We sang the naval hymn and laid a wreath and remembered those brave young men who had died.

A year later, in 2004, I was the commodore of the RNVR Yacht Club at the sixtieth anniversary of the D-Day landings when there was considerable ceremonial activity in France. I laid a wreath at the Naval Memorial at Oustreham a few days after one had been laid by His Royal Highness Prince Charles. In my speech to the local mayor and various French dignitaries, with their long waxed moustaches and tall banners, I announced in my best schoolboy French that we were there to remember those who had given their lives for freedom; that we must also remember all the French civilians who had been killed by the shelling and the damage which had been caused for the purposes of the Liberation.

The French Mayor had not heard this kind of speech from an Englishman before, obsessed as we usually are by remembering the war dead from our shores and from our allies. With tears streaming down his face, he publicly kissed me and invited us all to the *mairie* for a superb reception. Later we proceeded in single file under Pegasus Bridge which raised itself almost in salute as we sailed gracefully up the river, battle flags flying, to Caen for celebrations and remembrance.

On 21 October 2005, the 200th Anniversary of the Battle of Trafalgar, I commissioned my present boat, *Alana III*, which is a

Bavaria 42. I am deeply in love with this boat and talk to her regularly. She usually replies with a squeak but occasionally she says nothing in silent disapproval. Initially, I shared the boat with my brother, Patrick, but he eventually decided that his interest in vintage cars, including an Aston Martin and a Jaguar XK150, did not leave much time for sailing.

About the same time, I joined the Royal Southampton Yacht Club, largely because it has an outstation called Gins Farm on the beautiful Beaulieu River. Here club members can tie up their boats to the pontoon, have a superb dinner and stay overnight in tranquil and beautiful surroundings. I have been invited to deliver various speeches there.

On the occasion of the opening of the new and extended pontoon at Gins Farm by the Admiral of the Royal Southampton YC, His Royal Highness Prince Michael of Kent, I was asked by the commodore to give the vote of welcome to him and an audience of 200 people. Many of them were the great and the good who came to witness the solemn opening of this new pontoon. I noticed that many of the guests and other attendees were rather nervous and the atmosphere was rather intimidating. This was certainly not the fault of His Royal Highness; he was charming to meet.

Still, I decided that the atmosphere needed relaxing somewhat so I began my speech by saying, 'Your Royal Highness, My Lords, Commodore, Ladies and Gentlemen, on the way here I was on a train when an Irishman came down the carriage and asked, "Is there a Roman Catholic priest here?" There was silence. He then asked, "Is there an Anglican vicar on this train?" Again, there was no reaction. And so he added, "Is there a Rabbi here?" Still silence. Then a little man in a grey suit raised his hand and asked, "I wonder if I can help? I am a Methodist Minister." At this the Irishman said, "Oh no, no, no, you are no good at all, no good at all, all we are looking for is a corkscrew."' This was a joke I had picked up from Nicholas Parsons at the Athenaeum when he gave an amazingly amusing speech. It had the desired effect as everyone laughed.

But, of course, the secret of an anecdote like this is to weave it into the fabric of the speech. So I was able to go on to say and, of course, one thing the Royal Southampton Yacht Club does not lack are numerous corkscrews with which to welcome our guests and particularly our guests today.

I then went on more seriously to describe how unique Gins Farm is, situated as it is on the magical Beaulieu River. Lord Nelson's favourite ship, the *Agamemnon*, was built at Bucklers Hard further up the Beaulieu River and was towed down the river after her launch right past the land on which we were all standing. In World War II many landing craft left from the river and some did not return. Prince Michael then kindly came on board *Alana III* with the flag officers to have a light lunch which Pam had efficiently prepared. We brought some crystal glasses and a silk Chinese tablecloth down from London and served rather good champagne.

In 2009 my late friend of fifty years from Derbyshire, Ian Shuttleworth, advised I really ought to belong to the Royal Yacht Squadron, of which he was a member. I doubted this, pointing out that it was the most distinguished yacht club in the world and in order to join one had to be rather wealthy, a brilliant international trans-Atlantic type yachtsman and well connected. I felt that I fulfilled none of these criteria. But he persisted and I was taken to various formal dinners such as at Trinity House and met members, several of whom I found that I knew. I was hawked around and had to make sure I was always on my best behaviour. At one point, someone in the squadron considering my case, blurted out, 'But can he sail?' So I took various members to Poole and back to Cowes in a bracing Force 6 and managed to avoid a sandbank called 'The Trap' near Hurst Castle. All was well.

After that I was put up for membership. A candidate cannot apply himself; he must wait to be invited. Any candidate who tries to apply for membership has his application torn up into tiny pieces. I was very grateful for the support and encouragement of Brian

Wright, Paul Kennerley, Sir Anthony Evans, David Darbyshire, Rear Admiral Roy Clare, Commodore Peter Melson, Keith Topley, Martin Stanley and others. So in 2013 I joined the Royal Yacht Squadron with the great privilege of being able to wear the White Ensign on my boat. This privilege was granted by William IV, the sailor king, who noted how many yachts of members of the squadron had assisted the Royal Navy.

The squadron was founded on 1 June 1815 at the Thatched House Tavern in St James's Street in London which is now an HSBC Bank. So, on the 200th Anniversary date, 1 June 2015, we formally met there for our spring meeting and then adjourned for a wonderful dinner in St James's Palace.

I have become heavily involved in the squadron doing race officer duties both for the bicentenary celebrations and also in Cowes Week. For the bicentenary there was a Fleet Review with 180 boats on buoys laid just off Cowes and another twenty really large ships at anchor further out. This huge event had been planned for five years under the leadership of Commodore David Hughes RN. Our Admiral, His Royal Highness the Duke of Edinburgh, accompanied by the First Sea Lord and the present commodore, the Hon Christopher Sharples, and the Lord Lieutenant cruised up and down the ranks of shiny yachts. We cheered him as he passed and later we cheered again when HRH Prince Michael of Kent went by in a following ship. Then there was a church service, Beating the Retreat by the Royal Marines and a superb dinner in the castle, the headquarters of the squadron in Cowes.

For the week long bicentenary regatta I helped as a race officer. There were about a hundred boats from all over the world including the magnificent and beautiful J Class boats, so expertly sailed and a joy to see. I also arranged a formal lunch at the Athenaeum where former commodore and author Maldwin Drummond delivered a fascinating illustrated talk on the bicentenary of the Royal Yacht Squadron and its role in maritime history. The Hon. Christopher Sharples and his wife Gaynor graced the occasion.

The rallies the squadron organise are superb. The first one I went to was at Cherbourg, the Channel Islands and Roscoff on the North Brittany coast. All the events were closely organised with the members guided by the staff who had gone there in advance. I have had superb and widely experienced ocean racers as crew members on board *Alana III* such as Captain William Pennefather RN and Karenza Boscawen.

Another feature of squadron life is the interesting weekends run at the castle in Cowes, the headquarters. Each year there is a 'history weekend' which Pam and I really look forward to. On one such weekend one member gave an interesting lecture about a relative who had charged with the Light Brigade at Balaclava in the Crimean War. He survived as a trooper and subsequently became a general. The lecturer used not only personal correspondence from this brave man but also articles from *The Times* and original and early photographs. He mentioned one lovely vignette where Lord Cardigan who had led the charge had penetrated through the Russian guns and was about to be shot by a troop of Russian infantry under the command of Count Radziwill. But he stopped the soldiers shooting at Lord Cardigan because he said he remembered him well from London society. So Lord Cardigan survived.

Another talk was given by a brave colonel whose grandfather had been in the Royal Welsh Fusiliers. He showed photographs of six of the officers standing together in 1914; they were all brave and academically gifted. Every single one of them including the colonel's grandfather was killed, not by the end of the war but by the end of 1914. What a waste! The blood line of the country has never fully recovered from such terrible losses, including the local regiments like the Accrington Boys just mowed down by machine guns. This kind of lecture given with personal archives was deeply memorable and moving.

The staff at the squadron are so well trained and efficient. It is a real privilege to be a member with such a fine group who proudly and reliably raise the White Ensign at 8 a.m. and lower it at sunset. We all value the loyal and experienced staff. I am glad to say that, like the Athenaeum, women are now entitled to become full members and many women, great sailors and leaders of men, thoroughly deserve to become just such. The commodore, The Honourable Christopher Sharples, ensures that high standards of seamanship, etiquette, good manners and courtesy prevail. The secretary is the widely admired and respected Patricia Lewington who keeps the show on the road and on the water. The squadron is supporting Sir Ben Ainslie in his noble quest to win the Americas Cup and return it to England, where it surely belongs, in 2017.

In 2004 I became a member of another yacht club, The Deauville Yacht Club in northern France. This came about when we went there for a family holiday in *Alana II* and the commodore asked me to join as an overseas member. It was a real honour, so I did. We visit Deauville each year. One year with others I organised a 'Sea Horse Rally' to Deauville for eight royal yacht clubs. We enjoyed horse racing, golf and yacht races with some splendid dinners, including a memorable one at the Deauville Casino with the mayor. Over fifty boats attended. It is fun being a member as I receive regular emails in French asking me to race around the Cans the next weekend, which I have to decline.

There was one delightful story relating to the Royal Marines and us. Pam and I found ourselves in Deal thirty years ago and decided to visit the Royal Marine Barracks there where both our parents had been stationed. We arrived at the main gate and asked for admission. The guard told us we weren't allowed in because it was a military establishment. I explained that my father had been med-ical director and Pam had been brought up in House E. No good. I showed my RNR officer's ID card; still no entry. Then I added in desperation, 'Would it make any difference at all if I told you that I was conceived here?' The guard paused and then replied, 'Park over there Sir.' We were in. Pam even found the house with a faded

'E' over the front door. She remembered pushing a pram with a doll in it across the parade ground when the marines were being inspected. Her father, who was on parade himself at the time, was distinctly unamused.

14

BACK TO ENGLAND:
AN IMMIGRATION ADJUDICATOR

We returned to our Edwardian house in Putney after nearly seven years away. Richard started at the Falmouth College of Art to do a foundation course in graphic design while Alexandra began swotting for her A Levels at St Mary's. Susie was installed at Putney Park School, a prep school within walking distance of our house, while Pam went off to study for a year at the Hornsby International Dyslexia Centre to learn how to teach children with special needs. She eventually passed with good results which enabled her to start teaching in a private school.

Soon after we got back I went off to see Sir Tom Legg and others in the Lord Chancellor's Department. I suggested to them that they really didn't want me to come back and I didn't want to return myself. I thought that they rather too readily agreed that I should not return, though this was at least partly because a senior official would have had to be removed to make way for me. In any event, I was out of touch with civil service procedures.

I indicated that I would quite like to become what was then known as an immigration adjudicator because I had set up the organisation in 1987 and had been immersed in immigration and nationality law ever since. In my dealings with the Chinese and other countries, I had come to know such law well. I added that having visited fifty-five countries and negotiated with many of them, I had learned the humility to recognise that our complex system of law was not always right. In particular I had come to respect the sheer intellectual brilliance of many of the Chinese with whom I had worked in Hong Kong and so recognised that immigration could bring many benefits both to individuals and to the UK provided it was properly managed and controlled. Eventually, it was decided that I should retire from the Lord Chancellor's Department officially.

I called on His Honour Judge Pearl, always immensely courteous, in the Strand at the office of the immigration adjudicators which he led. The staff were kind enough to let me spend two days sitting in court and watching them deal with immigration appeals after refusals by the Home Office. With this experience and a lot of background reading I went before a board to become a part-time adjudicator.

In order not to be seen to be giving me a particular favour as I was a former colleague in the department, I was interviewed by a more senior and tougher board than was usual. The perceptive statutory lay woman from the north, who was not too kindly disposed towards me, asked what my politics were. I replied that I was 'an extreme –' and at that her government pencil scribbled with excitement, '– centrist.' The disappointed pencil fell sadly to the desk. In fact, my politics are undefined but I could never be to the left of Tony Blair or to the right of David Cameron.

I passed, but years later I was told by the chairman that I had not passed quite as well as I thought I had. I was appointed a part-time immigration adjudicator in order to assess my capabilities before I could apply to become a full-time salaried adjudicator. In October 2000, after two years sitting part-time, I was interviewed, given a written test and appointed a full-time salaried adjudicator. For this board I was relieved to be told I had done well.

This practice of part-time judiciary, having been introduced in Sir Derek Oulton's time in the Lord Chancellor's Department, served three purposes. First of all it provided part-timers who could assist the full-timers in the disposal of business; secondly it provided a cadre of potential candidates for full-time appointments when vacancies arose and thirdly it weeded out those who suffered from 'judgitis', the pomposity or rudeness that overcomes some people when sitting on the bench. It was surprising how many people became irritatingly pompous and annoying when given the power of running a court from the bench.

Soon after I started I was given a brief by some former colleagues in the department over lunch. They advised me that the adjudicators were notoriously lazy because they adjourned too much. I was told some of them were not of the highest intellectual calibre. So off I went to Hatton Cross, a large court centre situated under the flight path at Heathrow. The noise was indescribable although there was double glazing. I arrived as a judge convinced that I had a brilliant career already behind me.

There were twenty-six court rooms and numerous chambers for the judges to prepare cases and dictate judgments. I met the judicial leader and said I would like to meet the staff in order to find out what they did and work in close cooperation with them. I was advised rather stiffly that this was not appropriate because it was very much 'us' and 'them'. I could not believe this as I had been staff myself when I was running the law courts in the Strand. So I went to see the staff.

The look of astonishment and pleasure when I spoke to them and asked for detailed descriptions of their operations and thanked them, was obvious. Most of the staff were ethnic minority from the Indian sub-continent and some of them were very bright with post graduate degrees. They wished to work there rather than in central London because they were near to their families in places like Slough and Hounslow.

I had been told the judiciary were, in effect, bone idle. I was surprised and overjoyed to see that this was an entirely unfair description. Unlike district judges who tend to come from relatively similar backgrounds, the adjudicators at Hatton Cross consisted of diplomats who had been legally qualified, former Chief Justices in common law jurisdictions, people who had worked for the United Nations or the International Criminal Court in the Hague, former Queen's Counsel, retired senior partners of well-known law firms and those who had worked in immigration advisory centres. Some were from ethnic minorities. I was assigned to Esme Martins who hailed from Ghana and had vast experience of immigration law. She was my mentor and really remained so for the whole of my career. I was very fond of and grateful to her.

I also found out that the allegation that they were lazy because they adjourned too much was rubbish. Each day an adjudicator who was sitting had five cases to complete but the first two were 'for mention' cases, that is to say cases that would not be heard that day but for which directions were being given, like producing statements, to ensure that when the case was heard in about six weeks' time it could proceed. So these were not hearings at all, they were just directions hearings. Yet I found out that they were being recorded as adjournments. So every adjudicator had a two fifths adjournment rate before they had even started.

On learning this, I immediately telephoned a senior official in the Lord Chancellor's Department responsible for the adjudicators and we agreed to meet for lunch. During our meeting I explained how the recording system worked and how when I had challenged it at Hatton Cross I was told the computer was incapable of recording anything else, except an adjournment. The official whom I saw for lunch, spluttered over his soup, went pale and remarked, 'We have been misleading the Lord Chancellors for years.' So, far from being lazy or intellectually below par I found that the adjudicators were immensely hard-working; tough but fair and compassionate. In many cases they were exceptionally able and with very wide international experience.

Meanwhile, as part of my rehabilitation back into the UK I was kindly invited by the Lord Chancellor's Department to the Opening of the Legal Year Ceremony in Westminster. So I went to Westminster Hall with its great hammer-beamed roof dating back to Edward the Confessor for the reception in my morning coat, proudly wearing my only medal, the Reserve Decoration. I found myself purely by chance in a group of senior judges including two Lord Justices of Appeal and one law lord. Then Lord Mackay appeared. He was no longer the Lord Chancellor as there had been a change of government and Lord Irvine had succeeded him. I had previously worked for Lord Mackay and met him regularly; we got to know each other well.

As Lord Mackay approached and saw this group of about seven or eight people, the first thing he said was, 'Hello James, how nice to see you again.' This was such a kind gesture, typical of him. All the other far more distinguished people suddenly looked at me and wondered who on earth I really was.

At this time I was also elected to the Athenaeum. The first secretary in 1824, was Faraday and Sir Humphry Davy was an early member. It was founded mainly by John Croker, an MP and secretary to the Admiralty who was renowned as being autocratic. This led to the famous ditty:

> My name is John Wilson Croker,
> I do as I please,
> You asked for an ice-house,
> But I gave you a frieze.

This was the beautiful frieze around the outside of the club's magnificent building.

In order to join the Athenaeum I had to be proposed and seconded and then supported by a sufficient number of members who, firstly, knew my work and, secondly, knew me socially. In this way an applicant cannot simply buy himself into the club. I suppose my job as legal advisor, although carefully monitored, for the handover of Hong Kong sounded sufficiently prestigious for me to gather enough support. I enjoyed serving on the Talk Dinner Committee for six years and found some of the speakers. I chaired many dinners, with speakers including Sir David Tang, Sir Sherard Cowper-Coles, Sir Malcolm Rifkind, Rear Admiral Chris Parry, Lady Margaret Hodge, Magnus Linklater, Patrick Derham, Maldwin Drummond, Crispin Steele-Perkins, Tom Cunliffe and

Nicholas Parsons. It is a magnificent club with fine food and wine and witty male and female company. My father was a member before me.

One of the earliest friends I met there was Sir David Spedding. When I asked him how he got his knighthood, he replied that he had been in the security services. So I naughtily asked him if he had been 'M'. 'No,' he replied, 'C.' Sadly he died young.

15
IMMIGRATION APPEALS

Much of my work as an immigration adjudicator had to do with the immigration appeal system established in the UK back in the 1970s. This was set up to deal with appeals from adverse decisions of Home Office officials in England and entry clearance officers in embassies or high commissions abroad. A typical appeal might come from a Pakistani man who wished to assert his right to live in the UK after marrying his first cousin, a British citizen, in an arranged marriage. It consisted of appeals against refusal to allow family reunion, to be a visitor or a student or an investor in the UK. Later, asylum and human rights appeals predominated.

An applicant would apply to the Home Office or entry clearance officer at an embassy for immigration rights such as to visit, study, settle here, not be deported and, where that application was refused, a detailed letter of refusal was sent to the applicant. That applicant, now an appellant had a right of appeal to the immigration tribunal presided over by an independent judge like me.

In court the appellant would usually be represented by a lawyer, while the Home Office would be represented by a presenting officer or a briefed barrister. As the judge I would sit alone except in deportation cases where I would be accompanied by a lay member, usually a person of distinction, retired from the armed forces or a former diplomat or academic. I would welcome all parties and explain the procedure to the often frightened appellant. When the appellant was abroad, his case would be made by the sponsor, usually a close relative. Many were used to a vicious, corrupt, bullying and unfair court system in their homeland.

The appellant, who would have already been interviewed by the Home Office or usually an entry clearance officer, would be guided through the evidence by the appellant's own lawyer and then cross examined on behalf of the Home Office. Usually there would be an interpreter. There may be several witnesses. There were often huge bundles of background evidence about the claimed country of nationality. Then there would be closing speeches. I would usually reserve judgment contained in a written 'determination', often running to over fifteen pages. That determination had to be ready in two weeks. We were hard pressed.

Once when an enormous Egyptian woman appellant appeared in court, she said, before she sat down, the only English she knew, 'I have got my rights.' I replied that I wanted translated to her, 'Madam in my court you have your rights, which I am pleased to apply. But also you have an obligation and that is to tell me the truth.' Immediately all her relatives at the back of the court burst into laughter as she obviously had no intention to tell me the truth.

Many of the immigration cases when I joined concerned family visitors, that is to say people who said they wanted to visit family in this country for a short time. But the issue was whether that person would actually leave the UK at the end of the visit. Often the case was about a person from the Indian sub-continent who, for example, wished to attend a family wedding in Slough. If the appellant had visited before and gone back, that was a serious credibility issue in favour. If half of his family had arrived before and stayed on illegally in Slough, the Home Office would submit that the application just to visit was unfounded, especially if the appellant had just sold his shop and house in his homeland. The appellant would be abroad and represented by the sponsor, the person he wished to visit.

There were many cases involving students being enrolled in dodgy colleges. Sometimes the appellant was genuine but the college wasn't. Their whole village back home might have contributed to their receiving a good education in England only for the college to turn out to be an office with five computers, of which only three worked, despite 2,500 students being enrolled. Other times, the appellant knew perfectly well that the college was dodgy but wanted to use the visa to enter the UK and then disappear. In both cases the appeal had to be dismissed.

I had many interesting cases relating to au pairs including one where a Turkish construction worker tried to make out that he was going to be an effective au pair to a family in leafy Surrey. The elegant Surrey lady who had agreed to employ him thought he was female. Needless to say he lost his appeal.

There were issues about children, in particular whether the sponsor parent here had had sole responsibility for the financial and other support of that child back in the home country. If the sole responsibility including decisions relating to education, safety, clothing and religion were made by the parent here then the child could join the parent here, subject to a means test of the sponsor. But in many cases the responsibility was either non-existent or shared with a person in the home country. So entry clearance from the home country to the UK could not be allowed.

Before Poland became a member of the EU I had a case where an elderly ex-service Polish father wanted to bring his daughter over here to join him. The case was strong and the appeal was going to be allowed but I felt I could do some more good. I said to this proud old man that we could not forget the Polish Spitfire squadrons in the Battle of Britain or the Polish destroyers who slipped out of the Baltic and joined the Royal Navy. So I told him it was payback time. The appeal of his daughter would be allowed. He stood up and slowly and with great dignity saluted me; a great moment.

There were many difficult European Union law cases to decide including freedom of movement for workers. Turkey, in particular, offered many tricky cases because of its agreement with the European Union for workers to establish businesses in European Union countries, despite the fact Turkey is not a member of the EU. In those cases a proper business plan and a viable business had to be demonstrated. There was an impressive young Turkish couple who arrived with a detailed plan for a restaurant showing that a fair profit would be achieved. I was delighted to give such people their chance. But often the business plans were churned off a word processor by the same company from some industrial estate. They were of little help in most cases.

A major part of the work consisted of family proceedings, involving relatives reuniting in the UK and also marriages. One of the main requirements of the immigration rules legislation is that both parties intend to live with each other as spouse permanently. There were many cases during my time as an immigration judge of European men meeting attractive Thai girls on holiday, marrying them and wishing to bring them back to the UK. Having worked in the Far East I was well aware of this situation. With one such man I asked him whether he had given any money to the Thai family. He told me proudly that he had built them all a new long house. Knowing the usual scams, I asked him how many uncles had written to him asking for money for their eye operations. There were two of them. The girl worked in a bar and was very attractive. He was plainly in love with her but the correspondence from the other side showed a very determined gold digger of the first order.

In such cases it was difficult to produce the right judgment; the gentleman might curse me for dismissing the appeal of his wife, but in doing so I was saving him from being deserted, bereft and broken by a wife who would leave him after she had been issued with a visa and come to the UK. These were not pleasant cases but it was important to make a fair decision based on the evidence.

The rules also required the husband to be earning £18,600 a year before he could bring his wife into the UK. Many devoted couples sadly fell short of this. One of the last cases I decided before retirement consisted of a Chinese chef, originally from Beijing, who had been working in kitchens in the UK for eleven years, trying to earn enough money to bring his wife over from Beijing. This was not a sham marriage; they had been together thirty years. They corresponded regularly and she had learnt English. Yet he kept on being denied leave to bring his wife over owing to financial considerations.

I listened to his case most carefully. Then he produced an old moth-eaten savings book from a bank in Beijing showing that for many years he had been saving money in Chinese currency to the value of £25,000. The Home Office felt this document was not genuine or that his savings were not credible. I said I had worked in China or part of it, Hong Kong, for ten years and recognised the obsession with most Chinese for making savings because there was no proper pension system. That obsession applied to this couple. The chef agreed. The document was clearly genuine.

I told this chef I was going to allow his wife's appeal because I recognised he had been working in hot dangerous kitchens, probably with cockroaches running around for years to try to bring his wife in. They were obviously devoted to each other. I told him it was my pleasure to allow the appeal. Almost the last thing I remember before I retired was him standing there with tears streaming down his face as he gave me the deepest Chinese bow, as if prostrating himself before an emperor of the Ming dynasty. He did this in grateful thanks.

On the other hand there was a surge of sham marriage cases. The Home Office estimate 10,000 of these take place each year; which must be an underestimate. The cases that came before me were often very highly organised with girls from eastern European countries being brought in by coach and taken to a registry office to marry a gentleman, usually from North Africa. She would have right of entry being in the EU and so she could stay as his wife, and he with her, provided the marriage was genuine and both parties intended to remain with each other. When the formalities had been completed the girls would be put on the same coach and taken back to Eastern Europe.

The authorities in registry offices and the Home Office seemed remarkably slow at picking up what was actually and obviously going on. They were reluctant to challenge any of these marriages for, no doubt, reasons of diversity and cohesion. Only when the problem became so obvious and serious enough for it to gain a lot of media attention did the registrars start to inform the police and immigration authorities.

One such appeal that came before me consisted of a Polish girl who had married a man from Bangladesh, the latter being the appellant. When the police and immigration officers raided the matrimonial home they found the Polish lady sleeping next to a large Polish builder, not the Bangladeshi appellant. The appellant, it transpired, lived forty miles away. He was also found to have failed the toothbrush test; none of his personal possessions were in the matrimonial home. Both individuals were subsequently prosecuted. This kind of action was rare though, another example of poor enforcement of immigration rules by the Home Office.

There were many sad and at times deeply worrying cases of poorly educated men from the Indian sub-continent who had married bright Asian women from the north of England. The women were prized for their intelligence, beauty and above all because they had British passports. The woman would meet the man for the first time days before the wedding in India and, if she refused to marry, enormous pressure and indeed threats of violence and worse were made against her by her own family. So the marriage would go ahead and the husband would then apply to join his wife here. Further down the line the frightened but articulate wife would appear in court, deliberately without a lawyer, to say that she loathed her husband and could not support his application to enter the UK. Had I reiterated this in my judgment she would be done for.

In cases such as this I would protect her by finding other reasons for dismissing the appeal of the husband trying to get in here. There is a real problem over forced marriages among some in the Asian community and it is high time more effort was made through education and protection by social services and the police. When I saw terrified and courageous Asian women, who had effectively been raped on their wedding night, all I wanted to do was help them.

16

ASYLUM CASES

The bulk of the cases that came before me as an immigration judge were asylum cases. These were often very tricky. The role of the judge was mainly to decide whether the appellant was 'credible' or had invented a story. As a rule, each asylum case involves applying the definition of a refugee in the 1951 Refugee Convention and the European Union Qualification Directive to the individual. This runs as follows:

> A refugee is a person, who owing to a well-founded fear of being persecuted for reasons of race, religion, nationality, membership of a particular social group, or political opinion, is outside of the country of his nationality and is unable or, owing to such fear, is unwilling to avail himself of the protection of that country.

A person who is claiming to be a refugee but has not yet been found to be one is an asylum seeker, not a refugee. The press often get this wrong.

Of course, a person may have a well-founded fear of persecution for another reason. For example, a young and vulnerable woman who had been violated by a gold-toothed thug in prison may be in real danger of persecution on return but this does not fall under the Refugee Convention. In these kinds of cases the Human Rights Act incorporating the European Convention on Human Rights (ECHR) applies. Article 3 of the ECHR provides that no one shall be subject to torture or to inhuman or degrading treatment or punishment. So in that case the woman may lose under the Refugee Convention but win under Human Rights.

Many cases did involve persecution or harassment, but at local village level arising from issues such as land disputes. In these cases the appellant would not be granted asylum because they could, in fact, relocate safely to another part of the country. Asylum by definition is an international protection measure, to be granted only when an appellant cannot receive protection in their country of nationality.

This is an important point, particularly in relation to the recent migrant crisis; asylum is a noble measure to save the vulnerable from persecution. In theory, as soon as a migrant claiming fear of persecution has got to a safe country they should claim asylum there. Then that migrant should be fingerprinted and the asylum process begins. Asylum is not designed or intended to be a measure whereby a migrant may cherry pick which country they would like to go to.

The principle of first country asylum is enshrined in the Dublin Convention whereby if an asylum seeker arrives in this country but has been finger printed in the first safe country from which he absconds, the first country is supposed to receive back that asylum seeker from this country so that the asylum claim may be considered there.

Another of the many thorny issues to do with asylum cases was illustrated by a well-meaning report from a BBC journalist I saw not so long ago. The journalist was interviewing a refugee who had arrived in Calais after fleeing persecution from Boko Haram in Nigeria. His story was accepted at face value, yet he provided no details. Even if his untested story was true, Nigeria is an enormous country and Boko Haram, nasty though it is, operates in the north and east of this vast country. So this Nigerian would find it difficult to sustain a claim for asylum as he should be able to relocate to another and safe part of Nigeria. Asylum is a measure of international protection so where a migrant can relocate safely to another part of the country of nationality of that migrant, that is what the migrant is expected to do.

Each appeal before an immigration judge, if not adjourned, is followed by a written and detailed judgment, often running into many pages. This outlines the facts and applies these to the law, allowing the appeal or dismissing it.

I had many rewarding genuine asylum cases; one such matter involved a Sri Lankan man who said he had been viciously scalded at the hands of the Sri Lankan government. He was facing deportation and yet he had never been asked to show his injuries to his solicitor. There was no medical report. I asked him to show the court his injuries which he did with dignity. Both feet and his lower legs were hideously deformed by scalding. He could not have done this himself. The Home Office barrister was so appalled he conceded the appeal at once.

As an immigration judge you see first-hand man's inhumanity to man. I allowed appeals from Eritrea where so called national service could be slave labour for years. Eritrean cases are now growing in number. Tamils from Sri Lanka who were suspected of involvement with the Tamil Tigers were at risk of persecution. Journalists from any number of African dictatorships and those who publicly and bravely opposed President Mugabe were at risk. A person who had converted from Islam to another religion risked the death sentence in some countries. In many places where people demonstrated peacefully for fairer elections, less corruption and for human rights they were at risk of persecution.

I was also instrumental in taking the scandal of female genital mutilation (FGM) forward. In one such case an appellant from Guinea aged twelve had, according to the objective evidence, a ninety per cent chance of FGM on her return. The Home Office was seeking to return her to Guinea. The Home Office said she probably had already been subjected to FGM and so she should go. I adjourned for a consultant's report. She had not had it. I allowed the appeal and was the first judge to hold that she was a member of a particular social group under the Refugee Convention.

It is a disgrace that, to date, no prosecution has ever been successful in this country for FGM, which remains a massive and continuing problem. The perverted political correctness and over-reaching wish for community cohesion which has contributed to such scandalous inaction is similar to that which allowed the abuse in places like Rotherham to persist. Social workers, police and the medical services must be on the lookout for young girls at risk and then take preventive action like preventing the girl from leaving this country in the 'cutting season' and prosecuting elder members of families involved in such barbarism. In some cases I came across the cuts were so severe that infection had set in causing the girl to be infertile and in constant pain.

Every case had to be treated, as it were, from ground zero. It was tempting to stereotype appellants by concluding that every Jamaican was a Yardie, every Vietnamese was involved in cannabis production or every Albanian a pimp on an industrial scale. I was scrupulous in avoiding that lazy temptation. I had a case where a couple from Peru had claimed asylum. They were peasant farmers who said they had tried to organise resistance to the Shining Path terrorist group and had been driven from their farm. The husband told a story which could have been true but lacked bite and detail. His wife gave evidence separately; she had not heard the evidence of her husband. It was in such detail and corroborated her husband's evidence precisely. This was a shock to my complacency as I realised she was telling the truth. I allowed their appeals and the Home Office did not appeal my decision.

There were also many cases from Iraq. One unusual case was of an Iraqi lady who said she had been an interpreter for the Americans in the Green Zone in Baghdad. Her story was that she had been followed and harassed at her home. Eventually she was shot at while driving her car. She gave a coherent case. She even produced her American ID card, contract of employment and other extensive documentation. So I asked the blinking Home

Office representative whether anyone in the Home Office had, as they say in the Navy, 'engaged Mark 1 brain' and phoned the American Embassy in Grosvenor Square to check her out. Nobody had done so. I allowed her appeal and made an observation in my determination that Iraqis, who had interpreted for the British, may in some cases be at risk. The Home Office did not appeal my decision. I am still at a loss to understand why the government has been so slow to protect the Afghan interpreters left behind when our soldiers were withdrawn.

While trying to fight stereotypes the immigration judge also has to be very wary of the vast industry out there of people smugglers, agents and bent legal advisers taking advantage of appellants. One solicitor was found to have over a hundred blank Punjab University degree certificates to be filled in as needed. Some appellants themselves play the system. A Nigerian before me submitted a wanted poster of himself that he had clearly mocked up on a desktop publisher. Unfortunately, the date of it showed that by his own story he had already been in prison for six months; so he was hardly likely to be wanted when he was already in custody.

On another case, a Sri Lankan man claiming to be a Tamil fleeing persecution in Sri Lanka said he had escaped by boat before finding his way to the UK via Italy. I asked him to describe the boat and he said that it had six containers on it. He added it was about the length of the courtroom, about forty feet. I declared that I was a sailor and a former Naval Officer and could safely conclude that any ship of forty feet with six containers on it would go straight to the bottom of the harbour. He maintained that he had been on deck the whole time. He said that the ship did not stop for fuel or water and went the whole way to Italy without stopping. I asked him whether he had seen any land before he arrived in Italy but he had seen no land. I pointed out that if his story was true he would have passed through the Suez Canal where he could have almost leant over the side of the ship and collected sand to make sand castles with. He was plainly lying. It emerged that he had flown club class from Sri Lanka to Paris on his own passport and then come over on Eurostar with false documents and indeed, a false story.

Another of the major problems we came up against was to do with black Africans in the Sudan being attacked by the lighter skinned Arabs of the Janjaweed. The slaughter was awful; 200,000 had been killed. As a result of this we had a whole string of Sudanese cases claiming that they had been harassed on their farms by the Janjaweed. One such case was startling in that the Sudanese interpreter was deeply suntanned and lined but the appellant was fair skinned and with soft hands. He was clearly just an office worker from Khartoum.

Still, I asked him to explain the circumstances of his case. He said he had a farm with thirty-five cows and he had to sell the cows to get a flight from Khartoum to the UK. The Home Office barrister asked him how much each cow was sold for and the total was just ten per cent of the plane fare. The appellant then added, hastily, that he had some sheep but he managed to hide them from the Janjaweed on his farm even though he was raided twice a week. I suggested to him that sheep tended to make rather a lot of noise so it would be unlikely that the Janjaweed could have missed them. His whole case collapsed in a heap.

Before I retired there was a series of 'Failed Child Afghanistan Suicide Bombers' appeals. These were unaccompanied minors who had somehow been smuggled into this country. They claimed asylum. One typical case involved a boy who said he had been in a camp for two years learning about explosives and how to blow up targets. Then one day a vest was strapped on and he was directed to walk towards the British tanks. Just before he reached the tanks he had second thoughts. He ran away and soon saw a cow which he recognised belonged to his father. So over the hill he went to his father's farm where the whole village rejoiced and cut off his vest and put him on a plane to Heathrow.

Since he was only sixteen, I directed the Home Office barrister to be patient with him. But still the story fell apart. He couldn't remember where his father's farm was. In any case, had his story been true, his minder would have blown him up at the first sign of weakness. What a coincidence it was that the camp was just over his father's hill. Why should the village all risk the wrath of the nearby Taliban? If anyone in the security services here for a moment believed this concoction he would have been taken away to a safe house and debriefed so as to ascertain where the camp was, who trained him, what explosives were used and what the next target would have been. This had not happened. The cases were all remarkably similar, with a story learned by heart.

In these cases the appellant had nothing to lose by such lies and possibly something to gain. If he persuaded a gullible judge – and there were a few of them about – that he was telling the truth, he would be granted asylum. If the appeal was dismissed the Home Office would allow him to stay until he was eighteen. Then he would mount a human rights appeal to stay.

We had Kenyans trying to be from Rwanda or Somalia, Nigerians pretending to be from Sierra Leone or Liberia and many North African Arab speakers pretending to be from Iraq. There were many claimants allegedly from Afghanistan who were in reality from Pakistan. These days there are many, particularly from North Africa, who speak Arabic pretending to be from Syria. Many Ethiopians pretend to be from Eritrea. But all these cases had to be decided very carefully. When they realised their case wasn't going to be successful, some appellants pretended to be gay. Naturally this had to be taken seriously; we had to decide whether the appellant was indeed gay and, if so, whether he was at risk on return. This was never easy.

Another common case to come before us was that of restaurant workers from the Indian sub-continent who had come here either illegally or had over-stayed their visit or student visas and were then caught. They would claim asylum in order to try to stay here. Some were telling the truth but most had tried to learn their stories and they could not remember them. Many deliberately did not cooperate with the authorities by failing to disclose where they had actually come from because they had no travel documents. When I retired in 2014 about sixty per cent of all asylum appeals were like this, with the appellants arriving here or staying on illegally and then claiming asylum when picked up, desperately trying to stay here.

One of my first cases in the job involved a young woman in her mid-twenties from Sri Lanka who maintained she was as a Tamil being persecuted by the Sri Lankan government. She lived in a bedsit in Gravesend. I was relatively inexperienced and at the end of the case I told her I was going to allow her appeal but a judgment would follow. She looked absolutely appalled and horrified. I told her well-known barrister that she should cheer up as she had won. He swiftly ushered her from the court before I could change my mind.

After that I asked the experienced Home Office barrister what on earth had happened; he then told me she had been sending all her benefits back to the Tamil Tigers to fund their activities and she did not expect to win her appeal; what she'd wanted was to be removed at the British taxpayers' expense and sent to Sri Lanka where she would re-join the Tamils and be garlanded with flowers. By allowing her appeal I had sentenced her to her unhygienic bedsit in boring Gravesend.

Many of the cases were from Africa involving fear of various dictators. These all had to be very carefully considered because it was likely that in some cases they were desperate. There were many cases from Zimbabwe where teachers, who were perceived as threats to the Government because they were intelligent and could impart messages or propaganda, were genuine refugees. But of course inevitably there were those who would pretend they were teachers or members of the Movement for Democratic Change, the main opposition party. One appellant described himself as a university lecturer in economics and in cross examination it emerged he had not even heard of John Maynard Keynes or the monetary theory of government postulated by Milton Friedman. He was barely numerate.

There were many cases from the Indian sub-continent, mainly from Pakistan and Bangladesh, involving individuals who said they belonged to the wrong political party. These were always difficult cases to decide because when power changed in a country like Bangladesh scores would be settled.

There were also numerous cases of Christians being persecuted in places like Pakistan. Often a commercial dispute would escalate into a claim that the Christian had insulted the Prophet, resulting in serious risk. But these cases were easy to fabricate and regrettably many were. There is however a serious and largely ignored problem of Christians being regarded as 'infidels' by militant Muslims in some countries. The problem is serious in Pakistan, where churches are burned to the ground while the police look on. Even in India there is a similar problem of increasing intolerance.

It seems that the persecution of Christians in so many, mainly Muslim, countries is being addressed only by Lord David Alton and Justin Welby, the courageous Archbishop of Canterbury. Are contracts and arms sales really so important that such unacceptable conduct can be overlooked and we walk by 'on the other side'?

Iranians would claim to have converted to Christianity from Islam. A potential death sentence would follow. There was even a Christian church for Iranians situated conveniently near the Immigration headquarters in Croydon. It was doing thriving business! I remember several such cases where the appellant would say that he read the Bible twice a day and was a genuine convert. I declared my Christianity and asked one such appellant who St Peter was. After a pause he replied that he was the father of Jesus!

I had many genuine cases where I was privileged to allow the appeal. It sounds unprofessional, but an experienced judge would in effect be able to 'smell' a case from great experience and instinctively feel that this appellant was lying or telling the truth. But the evidence always had to be carefully weighed and considered. Instinct was not enough. I had several cases of young Indian women who had fled honour killings because they would not marry the man chosen by the family. Two of these cases involved trembling women who had fled to an Asian refuge in the Midlands. I wondered at the time why the police had not done more to protect them. I allowed the appeals, backed up by detailed medical reports, of these genuinely terrified women.

But many appeals were blatantly fabricated. These often came from Somalia where the appellant had been carefully coached into the clan structure because some clans did not have military support. There was one dreadful unfounded case like this where a woman turned up allegedly from Somalia to announce that she had to flee because her husband had been murdered on the doorstep of her house in Mogadishu. She claimed to have found his body when she returned from doing the shopping. He had been killed by the local war lords, she said.

The Home Office barrister who, somewhat unusually, was well-briefed, got her to repeat the story and confirm that it was true, in particular that it was her husband who had died. Then he said to her that there appeared to be a problem; according to Home Office records her husband had come to England eighteen months earlier and claimed asylum. There was a stunned silence in court. The appellant's mouth opened silently like a cod caught unawares in the North Sea. Eventually, this lady said that there appeared to have been a mistake. We all agreed on that.

It was only when I was writing the judgment that I noticed another twist; the same firm of solicitors had acted for the husband as had acted for her. Accordingly, they knew perfectly well that the detailed statement they had drafted for her was a load of rubbish and deceitful. Needless to say I reported them to the Law Society. After six months I rang the Law Society to ask what they had done and got the pathetic reply that, as she had been told to leave the country as soon as she received my judgment and had done so, she could not be interviewed. But it was not necessary to interview her as all the information the Law Society needed was set out in that formal court judgment. The Law Society official added that no damage had been caused to the country by this case. I pointed out that this firm of solicitors had attempted to pervert the course of justice. The Law Society, disgracefully, took no further action against that firm.

There were, however, many devoted and professional firms of solicitors trying to help appellants but the legal aid budget was drying up. Some such firms were working at a loss and eventually had to close. So I had more and more litigants in person as they could not get legal aid. These appeals took longer as the judge had to be especially careful to enable that appellant to present the case clearly.

A piece of research often revealed that an appellant was lying. One glamorous and fur-coated lady who brought her similarly clothed children to court maintained she was a Palestinian who had fled persecution in a filthy Lebanese refugee camp. Her story was inconsistent. As the Home Office had failed to send a representative, I printed out details, photos and information about this camp from the internet during the lunch interval. Back in the court room I asked the appellant to describe this camp, the hygiene, running water, a medical centre and schools. She got everything wrong. I gave the print out to her lawyer and adjourned for half an hour so that he could take instructions on this new information. She was therefore given a chance to react to it. I offered an adjournment to another day. He returned to withdraw from the case. Honourably, he said that his new instructions were utterly inconsistent with the previous ones. She was, of course, not a Palestinian but a Lebanese who had deserted her husband and come to England with the children to enjoy a life here largely at the expense of the British taxpayer.

Some of these asylum cases could have political ramifications. When I first started, the civil war in Kosovo was in full flight and the news was full of pictures of Muslims fleeing from Kosovo after being bombed by the Serbs. Many of these people ended up in the UK; it was deeply upsetting. The real problem for us was that so many other people jumped on the bandwagon. Many of the people claiming asylum were not from Kosovo at all but ethnic Albanians from Albania. It was very difficult for an immigration judge to try to establish the facts. However, that is what is required in asylum cases, to establish the facts and then apply the law to those facts. Every case had to be decided on its own merits and carefully so, but sometimes those merits were very thin indeed.

There was a distinction, of course, between genuine asylum seekers and economic migrants coming to the UK to take advantage of the generous benefits, including housing and education for the children. There is nothing inherently wrong of course in being an economic migrant. Everyone is entitled to try to better themselves and the life of their family but an economic migrant cannot properly try to achieve this by suggesting that they are, in fact, a genuine refugee.

Asylum cases had to be taken very seriously because, if a judge got it wrong, the appellant could be put at risk. I was acutely aware that I was not a district judge in a county court arguing about the price of building work or a pair of jeans; in some cases I was responsible for a person's life. I took none of my cases lightly.

17

DEPORTATION APPEALS

One of the major and most complex areas of the law concerns the deportation appeals of foreign criminals and the application of Article 8 of the European Convention on Human Rights. In my experience these were mainly non-European Union cases; it's incredibly difficult to deport an EU citizen and this can only really be done on grounds of public security or public policy. The general philosophy is that the EU is a club so bad apples remain where they fall.

I had many cases of Jamaican Yardies involved in drug dealing and gang violence. In such cases, the tribunal may even take into consideration a nexus of long term poor behaviour, gang associations and even a pattern of rape allegations where the appellant had been acquitted of rape. Great care had to be taken in these cases to be fair to the appellant.

Deportation could take place for a non EU citizen where deportation was deemed 'conducive to the public good'; in other words if the appellant was a serious criminal and the public deserved protection. The law provided that where an appellant had been sentenced to twelve months imprisonment or more deportation was automatic. However, this proved less final than it sounds. The appellant was likely to argue that even though the sentence was for at least twelve months his human right to family life and the rights of his close family would be breached if he were to be deported.

I had many cases involving Jamaican Yardies where the appellant had secured 'Dear Daddy' letters in prison from a child they'd fathered during a previous relationship. It was argued on behalf of the appellant that this child would miss the fatherly example and leadership of the appellant and the appellant would miss his child. These cases usually got pretty short thrift on appeal. But it was surprising how courteous and charming many of these Yardies were in court.

Deportation appeals were usually straightforward on the deportation merits so most appellants concentrated on the human rights of themselves and their family under Article 8 of the European Convention on Human Rights (ECHR) to try to trump the legislation on deportation. Here the problems were difficult. Article 8 of the ECHR is widely misunderstood. This provides that:

> Everyone has the right to respect for his private and family life, his home and his correspondence. There shall be no interference by a public authority with the exercise of this right except such as in accordance with the law and necessary in a democratic society in the interests of national security, public safety or the economic wellbeing of the country, for the prevention of disorder or crime, for the protection of health or morals or for the protection of the rights and freedoms of others.

In other words the right to family life is a qualified and not an absolute right. The problem with the application of Article 8 identified by the acclaimed historian and brilliant Supreme Court judge, Lord Sumption, in a recent lecture, is that the straightforward provision for family life has been extended to cover matters never envisaged in the ECHR such as criminal sentencing and votes for prisoners.

I recognised when I was sitting that a judge must have the common sense and humility in deportation cases to consider the rights of the next victim of a violent thug pleading his human rights before me. Some judges engineered an unhealthy clash between the judiciary and Parliament in failing to secure the rights and freedoms of others set out in Article 8, as due to their simple consideration of the human rights of the appellant and his family only. The apparent arrogance of some judges at the bargain basement end of the judiciary is to seek to impose their narrow consideration of human rights, contrary to the democratic process. Feeling sorry for an appellant is not always a legitimate reason for allowing an appeal. But the Court of Appeal now has given helpful guidance to those lower down. In the case of 'LC China' in 2014 it held that the starting point for an Article 8 claim is, 'The recognition that the public interest in deporting foreign criminals is so great that only in exceptional circumstances would it be outweighed by other factors.'

There is a tension, and it should be a healthy one, of the government trying to protect us all from terrorism and crime on the one hand, and the courts ensuring that the government stays within the law on the other. This is a balancing exercise and it isn't easy. We do not want to live in a police state. The courts must also show public awareness as well as humility. This does not always happen.

It is important in a deportation appeal where, for example, an appellant has killed someone, to be fully aware of the sorrow and sadness that the victim's family have had to endure. One such case that came before me involved a Nigerian man who had killed someone outside a nightclub in a fight. The man had a distinguished record of academic excellence with sound references; he just happened to have been provoked and punched the person who was harassing him. With just one punch the victim fell to the ground and hit his head on the pavement. Subsequently he died.

The Nigerian man was convicted of manslaughter and sentenced to more than twelve months in prison. The Home Office wanted to deport him. It was a very difficult appeal where I sat with a lay person. We eventually decided to allow the appeal on human rights family life grounds owing to the record of this Nigerian, who had lived in the UK for many years and his great remorse. But we went to considerable trouble to explain our reasons in the judgment and expressed great sympathy to the victim's family so that that family would understand the reasons for allowing the appeal even if they didn't agree with the decision. The Home Office understandably appealed but our decision was upheld. Sometimes I do wonder whether we got that one right.

Some immigration judges, clever though they are, produce academic judgments worthy of a university thesis but don't possess that common touch to recognise that in many of our cases there are victims, whose feelings have to be recognised and respected. Article 8 of the ECHR is often applied by some judges as a sort of trump card to allow an appellant to remain even though that appellant has lost the asylum or deportation case. The second part of that article referring to the 'rights and freedoms of others' is very often ignored by judges. A Yardie may be successful in a deportation appeal but is very likely to get involved in drug dealing and associated violence again and thus have a detrimental effect on the rights and freedoms of others in this country if he were allowed to stay here. But every case has to be treated on its own merits.

18

COUNCIL OF IMMIGRATION JUDGES

In 2003, owing partly to my previous experience in Whitehall, I was elected in a contested election as the president of the Council of Immigration Judges for England, Wales and Scotland. By this time the whole enterprise had become vast. There were about 450 full-time immigration judges and 500 part-time judges in an operation costing about £2 billion a year in accommodation, staff running costs and salaries.

I found myself dealing with the late Mr Justice Hodge who was the president of the whole tribunal, our judicial leader. He had been the best president that the Law Society never had. He was very tactile and charming and a former student at Balliol College, Oxford. Occasionally, we disagreed, partly because he wanted to control the judges more and to ensure that the work was completed on time. I felt in my capacity as president that there was too much emphasis on speed and quantity and not enough on quality. There was a real tension between the Council of Immigration Judges and the administration by civil servants because adjournment rates were being measured and even at one time, before it was stopped, the numbers of appeals allowed or dismissed by a particular judge were recorded.

I secured a name change from 'adjudicator', which made us sound like parking adjudicators, to 'judge'. There was also tension over the time deemed necessary to write judgments after hearing up to three appeals in one day. I called for the implementation of a 'writing up' day. When the administration instinctively resisted this, independent consultants were brought in at my request. They recommended that one day was often not enough. So we got our day and the quality of the judgments rose as a consequence; there were fewer appeals from the immigration judges too.

I was wrong on one initiative implemented by Henry Hodge, and that was judicial appraisal. When it was first suggested, we were given a lecture by some ghastly officials from the Cabinet Office on a national training course which explained how appraisal worked in the civil service. It was all about quantity and disposal of business and measurements of that sort to determine whether the organisation had been successful. There was no measurement of quality or even interest in it or recognition of the importance of judicial scrutiny with every case different in length and complexity.

I felt that this system would not be appropriate for the judiciary. I was wrong on this because the appraisal system introduced by Henry was actually useful and to me personally. Each one of us was appraised by a more senior judge each year. We had to send some previous judgments to this senior judge and they would then sit in court all day. They would watch how we conducted the cases and dealt with applications for adjournment, how we handled difficult appellants and lawyers and how we treated the appellants. We would send the judgment of each case to this judge so they could see how thorough or not we had been. That appraisal judge could not however change the decision, which remained with the judge being appraised. As we sat alone, except for deportation cases when we sat with a lay person, it was actually very helpful to have a more senior judge there to give advice. In one or two cases, not in mine, a judge was found not to be fully up to speed and was recommended for further training. At first sight, appraisal seemed to be an interference with judicial independence. But it turned out to be a useful initiative and I benefitted considerably from it.

I had to admire much of the work of Henry Hodge who, with his political contacts, certainly gave greater authority to our juris-diction as a whole. Sadly he died suddenly. His wife, Margaret, was the formidable Chair of the House of Commons Public Ac-counts Committee. When she came to the Athenaeum to give us a scintillating speech at a dinner which I chaired, I wore my Law

Society tie in honour of Henry, who had recently died. She was truly touched.

As president I was invited to the Home Office to see the immigration minister, Beverley Hughes, who was thoroughly decent, competent and honest in her work. She was eventually shafted inadvertently by her own officials, after she 'misled' Parliament about one-legged Romanian roofers getting visas with no difficulty. I explained to her and her officials what actually happened on the ground in the tribunal but made it clear that as a judge, policy was not for me but for her, an elected member of Parliament and a minister. I was delighted when she was elevated to the peerage.

I also had to appear before the Top Salaries Review Body to justify the status and salary of immigration judges. That body chaired by the renowned Michael Beloff, QC, was searching but fair and we won our claim.

As part of my duties I arranged the annual dinner of the Council of Immigration Judges at the Savoy. I was honoured by the presence of Baroness Butler-Sloss who was my principal guest and spoke so well. She had been particularly kind to me when I was chief executive of the Royal Courts of Justice and she was a Lady Justice of Appeal. I used to go to see her in Chambers with her black Labrador by the fire asking her for advice on judicial administration in those difficult times. In my capacity as president I went to Lord Hailsham's funeral and was seated in the VIP area of a packed St Paul's Cathedral. I was privileged to be there to honour my former and much revered Lord Chancellor.

19

THE QUALITIES OF AN IMMIGRATION JUDGE

In Proverbs it is said that, 'It is the fault of wise men that fools sit on Judicial benches.' The first quality of a judge is not to be a fool. Maturity and gravitas are what is required and those qualities do not always come with age. Sometimes a judge may feel that he or she is holding a dignified line between two squabbling parties: the appellant and the lawyer on the one hand and the Home Office on the other. At such moments, humour can sometimes cool things down. I remember on one occasion the two counsel both stood up and started shouting at each other. Everyone, counsel, appellant and interpreter were of ethnic minority background. So I invited them to calm down by saying, 'Come on we are all immigrants here.' They looked at me in astonishment. I continued, 'my grandfather came here as a doctor from Ireland in 1910.' They all smiled. The appeal continued in a professional manner.

A judge must not take over the cross examination but can ask questions to clarify the issues. Crucially, the judge must always be seen to be impartial. On one occasion there was an appeal against me as it was alleged I had 'descended into the arena' and asked too many questions. I had asked just thirteen questions and in a quiet, non-threatening manner. The appeal was dismissed. I was upheld but it was a warning to me. The famous litmus test is that both parties leave the court content that they have had a fair hearing.

It is important for a judge, even in unmeritorious cases, to be kind, charitable and compassionate to those involved. As Seneca observed, invective against a man in his trial is disgraceful. One cannot blame half the world for wanting a better life but that is not sufficient reason in law for a person to be allowed to enter or stay here. Being kind and compassionate does not mean that the judge must leave common sense at the door of the court and be gullible and frankly stupid on the bench. There is a vast industry out there of people smugglers, agents and bent lawyers taking advantage of appellants. Some appellants play the system themselves.

The judiciary must find the facts in a fair manner, without bias or rudeness and carefully apply the complex law to those facts mindful of the wider responsibility to the community. The judge must be briefed and well aware of the current political and human rights situation in the appellant's home country.

Judges must also apply the rule of law as described by Professor Dicey 150 years ago. This is the absolute supremacy of the law as opposed to the exercise of arbitrary power. 'Be ye ever so high, the law is above you,' as Lord Denning observed. This also includes equality before the law. As the much missed and great member of the Athenaeum Lord Bingham outlined, the law must be accessible, predictable and clear. Where a minister has been granted a discretion, that discretion must firstly be exercised and secondly exercised with reasoned justification. The law must be imposed without prejudice and fairly on all. Finally, Lord Bingham declared that the rule of law must afford adequate protection of fundamental human rights such as the right to life and to protection from torture. The rule of law does not mean rule by lawyers.

The judiciary must also apply the rules of natural justice. As Lord Ellenborough noted 200 years ago, a man cannot be condemned before he has been heard. He must know the case against him. The appellant must be given an opportunity to put his case. But it is not even as simple as that. Judges do not merely discover legal principles concealed in the undergrowth of ancient principle, legislation and confusing and inconsistent case law; they can also make law themselves within broad limits determined by statute and legal policy. During the case of Spectrum Plus before the then House of Lords, Lord Nicholls said: 'Judges have a legitimate law-making function. For centuries judges have been charged with the responsibility of keeping the law abreast of current social conditions and expectations.'

The responsibility of a judge is to apply the law impartially, fairly and carefully. It is rare, notwithstanding the observations of Lord Nicholls, that a judge actually makes new law. If that does happen Parliament usually catches up and legislates for it by statute law.

In my time as an immigration judge I found that courtesy counted and was appreciated. When I saw an appellant before me – even one who was lying – I always treated that person with courtesy. Sometimes they felt the judge was a fool who didn't notice what was going on. As a result, a lying appellant would relax too much and forget his lines. I ensured that I pronounced the foreign name of an appellant properly, invited the appellant to have a glass of water, relax and tell his or her story. If it was Ramadan I would hear the Muslim case first before the fasting appellant became too tired.

Preparation was always essential. One day I got two student appeals muddled up and asked one of the appellants to describe his economics course at the University of Sunderland only to find he had been studying engineering at Leeds! After apologising to counsel and to the appellant I never made that mistake again.

The judge should walk into court in a measured and calm manner and not give the impression of one swamped by papers. It was preferable not to trip up on the step to the bench. A bow to those assembled who were all watching the judge intently and a 'good morning' was always appreciated. It is not the purpose of a judge to dismiss all appeals and 'kick them all out' as I am often told during social occasions when it's discovered what I did for a living.

The role of a judge is to deliver a full and fair decision in accordance with the law. But the failure of the Home Office to enforce our decisions and remove most failed appellants was lamentable. Indeed, a few years ago an official from the Home Office actually informed a Commons Select Committee that the Home Office did not pursue failed asylum seekers for resource reasons. A recent report by the chief inspector of borders found that the Home Office had lost over 10,000 failed asylum seekers and a further 30,000 failed asylum seekers had not been removed over two years after all appeal rights had been exhausted. My feeling is that these figures are an underestimate.

It has been observed in jest that the main requirements of an immigration judge are a bizarre blend of relentless enthusiasm, burning faith and detachment, from reality. The judge dismisses an asylum appeal, the appellant lies low and then is made a British citizen six years later. Indeed, the Home Office makes 200,000 new British Citizens a year, which some see as a form of unofficial amnesty to reduce the number of illegal immigrants in the country. This failure to enforce decisions not only brings the tribunal into disrepute but the administration of justice itself. Indeed, this became clear when I had to refuse bail to a Somali who had been in the UK for just eight years yet had sixty-four previous convictions. He never thought action would be taken against him. I refused bail on the grounds that he was likely to abscond and put the public at risk of reoffending.

Bail hearings were a significant part of the immigration judge's duty. They took place when an appellant had been detained prior to removal. Bail could only be refused if an appellant was likely to abscond or reoffend. If an appellant was not going to be removed reasonably soon, say within a few months, bail had to be granted. There was therefore an incentive for the appellant not to cooperate. The application for bail was presented by a lawyer backed up by two sureties who would pledge usually several thousand pounds that the appellant would not abscond. The surety did not have to deposit that money, just show it was available. Often this failed when suspicious deposits were made into the bank account of the surety the day before the hearing.

These bail hearings were often very emotionally charged, with the distraught mother of the appellant at the back of court. At the end of the hearing the judge had to deliver a detailed oral judgment one way or the other. There was a presumption in favour of bail. Where an appellant was at risk of absconding or reoffending, bail could be granted if the appellant surrendered the passport and agreed to be tagged so that his whereabouts would be known. Tagging would also require a curfew. Bail involving a decision on the freedom of an appellant was indeed a very onerous task, not to be taken lightly.

In addition to finding the facts from often inadequate evidence, a judge also has to try to master complicated and ever-changing law. The legislation passed throughout the time I was on the bench became more and more complex while the drafting of the subordinate immigration legislation, the Immigration Rules, also became increasingly intricate and difficult to decipher.

Sometimes applying the law could become a real nightmare. Thankfully we were extremely well trained. There would be courses every year where the law would be brilliantly explained by such senior lawyers as Mark Ockelton, a deputy High Court judge. We would be given scenarios to discuss in small groups. We would then suggest a considered solution where we would be corrected by carefully considered answers from the expert training team. Throughout my career on the bench, the training was at times magnificently helpful. It was a great credit to the judicial authorities who organised it.

It was important to deal with all cases with compassion. The leading cases of 'N' and 'D v St Kitts' held that a person who had HIV was not entitled to stay in the UK unless to remove that person would in effect kill him. It had to be kept in mind that each HIV case was costing the taxpayer at least £25,000 a year in drugs alone and that is to say nothing of benefit payments. I had one case where the appellant was obviously seriously ill, shivering and perspiring at the same time in a courtroom where the air conditioning had been put on far too high and could not be reduced. He was wearing just a tee shirt so I adjourned the case for five minutes, returned to my chambers and gave him my sweater in order to keep him warm. This was greeted with astonishment by some of the court staff. But it was essential to assist this appellant so he could relax as much as was practicable and give his evidence without being too uncomfortable.

In a similar manner a young Iraqi man appeared before me a few years ago in tears. He had been abandoned by his lawyer and had managed to get a train from somewhere near Croydon to Feltham. But he had no money for the return journey and little idea how to get back to his bedsit. I asked him to turn out his pockets and indeed he only had about fifty pence left. He was representing himself. He was all alone and desperate. I asked the Home Office representative what would happen to him and received the unhelpful reply that he would be removed from the court and left to his own devices. I asked this man to wait and at the end of the court hearing I drove him to Feltham Station, bought the railway ticket for him and sent him on his way. This was perhaps an overemotional and ill-advised thing to do. But he could not speak English and I could not speak Arabic so it was impossible to discuss his case. In the end I had to reject his appeal but I made a recommendation to the Secretary of State that he be given exceptional leave to remain. There is more to a judge than being a note taker.

Every now and then a judge sitting on the domestic bench has the chance to do an act of real kindness; it is a privilege to be able to do so. Years ago I had a seventeen-year-old Jamaican appellant who had come into the UK with an aunt who said the appellant was her daughter. For various technical reasons she could not succeed in her deportation appeal but she had done brilliantly at GCSEs and was doing A-Levels with a place at university. I said in open court that I had been to Jamaica and I recognised the grim life she would be forced to lead with all that acquired education in London lost. I said that I had a seventeen-year-old daughter too, also doing very well but with great advantages. I invited the Home Office barrister to ask his boss to reconsider the decision to remove her. He came back twenty minutes later to announce that the Home Office would concede the appeal now. Everyone in court burst into tears. I wonder where she is now and whether she remembers that softhearted judge, who was privileged to give her a chance in life.

With some reluctance I decided to retire in 2014 after sixteen years as an immigration judge. I could have gone on to the age of seventy in 2016, but found the appeals increasingly complex. Writing a judgment proved to be a subtle game of croquet, so many hurdles to overcome to prevent a successful appeal from being mounted. I was also diagnosed with prostate cancer and the hormone treatment made me quite fatigued in the afternoons. My judicial leader, Donald Conway, kindly arranged lighter lists for me, when I was receiving treatment. I felt that with the passage of time I may not be as effective as I once was, rather like a Test cricket fast bowler who has to recognise the time to hang up his boots. Go out on top form so colleagues, lawyers and appellants remember the achievements of the judge and not the faltering mistakes that might come later.

Three of my cases even went all the way to the European Court of Human Rights in Strasbourg but I was upheld each time. I only had five of my cases overturned in sixteen years by an Upper Tribunal. I could be overturned only for an error of law which materially affected the decision. Three of these cases were clearly wrongly decided by the Upper Tribunal in that there was no error of law by me, just a different conclusion about the result! But in two cases I had got it wrong. In one of them I had thought the work permit was for one year when it was for five years with different criteria. That was careless. I was never overturned by the High Court, Court of Appeal or Supreme Court, which was a relief. This was due to hard and careful work but also due to the excellent training we all received and perhaps some luck.

I did not receive much official thanks for my time on the bench, just a standard three line letter drafted by some civil servant. When you retire in the public service you are soon forgotten. But when I retired from the RNR I got a three page letter from a senior naval officer in the admiralty. When I ran the law courts and a clerk retired after twenty years' service, that clerk received a personal testimonial from me on vellum so that it could be framed and proudly displayed to family and friends. These things are important.

Still, my colleagues were kind. Ninety of them gave me a superb farewell dinner attended by Pam and Richard, Alexandra and Susie at the Athenaeum. I gave a speech and was profoundly moved. I took down my pictures, packed up my beloved books and Chinese carpet and put them in the boot of the car. I gave cakes to the staff, thanked them quietly and then drove away.

20
HUMAN RIGHTS

Human rights has become an emotive subject. Many feel that appellants in courts are escaping the proper consequences for their actions, like deportation, by insisting on human rights to a compliant and sometimes out of touch judiciary. This has, in turn, been compounded by the migration crisis in Europe and the perception by some that the UK cannot control its own borders. Still, there is a great ignorance of human rights and a widespread feeling that Europe is interfering with our domestic law and legal independence by the application of badly decided cases on human rights law. This ignorance is especially obvious in the debate on whether the UK should leave the EU.

The European Convention on Human Rights (ECHR) is not a European Union piece of legislation; it is derived from the much larger Council of Europe based not in Brussels but Strasbourg. The UK government was a significant drafter of it. Most of the ECHR was incorporated into UK domestic law by the Human Rights Act 1998. Section 2 of the 1998 Act provides that courts and tribunals must 'take into account' the jurisdiction of the European Court of Human Rights. In other words the courts in this country are not actually bound by cases from the European Court of Human Rights. But the appellate judges in the House of Lords held in 2007 that decisions of the European Court of Human Rights were likely to be 'highly persuasive.'

The effect on immigration matters by this court where the UK government has lost cases is actually fairly limited to cases denying deportation. The view held by some that the Court of Human Rights grossly interferes with our daily lawful lives is not actually accurate. The case of Soering in 1989 held that deportation cannot take place if the appellant would receive human rights violations like torture on return. Another case held that various little-known Home Office policies were directed to be incorporated into the Immigration Rules so appellants knew what law or practice was being applied. No one can dispute that.

The court's jurisprudence leaves a 'margin of appreciation' in applying the Human Rights Convention to take into account local conditions or needs. In immigration terms there are two kinds of rights in the ECHR. The first of these, absolute rights, cannot be qualified and includes the right to life and freedom from torture or ill treatment. In 1996 it was held that the UK government could not extradite an alleged Indian terrorist to India as the appellant would be at risk of torture or worse on return. The other kind of rights in the ECHR are qualified rights, concerning matters such as family life and freedom of religion. Here the rights and freedoms of others must be balanced with the rights of an individual. The main cases to have riled the general public and the government are those concerned with matters such as allowing prisoners to vote. These are not immigration matters at all.

As a matter of gentle comment it does seem odd that the government, or some parts of it, is crying out for the ECHR to no longer be applied to the UK and for the UK to have its own Human Rights Act. I say this because any local Act would have to contain similar provisions as freedom from torture and protection of family life and freedom of religion in similar, if not identical, terms as the present law. To withdraw from the ECHR would set an awful appearance of intolerance to other members of the Council of Europe and indeed worldwide.

In immigration terms, a way forward may be to emphasise by statute and examples that the principle of proportionality allows UK courts to be more robust than merely 'taking into account' decisions of the European Court of Human Rights. So by statute, firm guidance would be given by the democratically elected Parliament to judges on how to interpret human rights law. While I have not seen the full facts surrounding one particular case that has made headlines in the UK in recent years, it does seem odd at first sight that a Libyan alcoholic with more than seventy-five previous convictions in the UK could not be deported to Libya on human rights grounds as he would not be able to enjoy a pint or two there. The consequence is that this country has to support this appellant through public funds and take the risk of further offending because his human rights would otherwise be thought to be breached.

So in my view we should not throw the baby out with the bath water. A way ahead without receiving international criticism may be to guide the judiciary, particularly the junior judiciary, into well considered decisions with guidelines which do indeed consider and apply the rights of others and not merely allow an Article 8 case to trump the Home Office.

A significant problem has been the cynicism of the public whenever human rights are mentioned. They are widely seen as a means by which the undeserving can trump a decision of a minister or to drive a coach and horses through the democratic will of an elected Parliament. A good example of this has been the extraordinary view of a UN committee that Julian Assange, who fled to the Ecuador embassy, has somehow been 'arbitrarily detained unlawfully' there. The committee itself consisted of representatives from Benin, Togo and Mexico, countries not exactly renowned for their human rights record. No wonder our Foreign Secretary described the ruling as ridiculous; Assange had fled to the embassy to avoid legal action in Sweden over an alleged rape case. He was and is free to leave the embassy at any time.

Another twist on the human rights debate is that even if the UK opted out of the European Convention on Human Rights, we would still be bound by a Charter of Fundamental Rights from the EU. These rights are wider than in the ECHR. For example, Article 7 of the EU Fundamental Rights Charter provides for protection of family life. But it does not contain the qualification or restriction in

Article 8 of the ECHR that the exercise of family rights are subject to 'the rights and freedoms of others.' Disputes on this charter are decided by the European Court of Justice in Luxembourg, not the European Court of Human Rights in Strasbourg.

The previous Labour government obtained an opt-out so that this Fundamental Charter, which is wider than the ECHR would not after all be binding on the UK. But a recent case about an Afghan asylum seeker was heard at the EU Court of Justice which held that this opt-out had actually no legal binding force. So this EU court can trump any ruling by our domestic courts, including the Supreme Court. The true effect in practice of this is awaited. One way to avoid rulings from the EU Court of Justice is to leave the EU. Another way is to persuade the Court of Justice not to intervene so much but to give domestic courts more leeway to take into account local conditions, culture and laws. So unnecessary interference should be avoided. The European Court of Justice should allow EU member states more 'margin of appreciation' to apply their own law and traditions.

21

ENFORCEMENT
AND DEPORTATION

In December 2014 it was revealed that among 1,859 of the most serious foreign offenders in the UK, 775 were murderers, 587 rapists and a further 155 convicted of raping a minor. Other serious offences included 200 sex offences against children, ninety-nine cases of manslaughter and fifteen terror offences. Foreign nationals convicted of sixteen murders and fifty-two rapes had been released from prison and were living in the community as the Home Office tried to deport them. The figures showed that the Home Office's foreign national case load featured 11,719 people including more than a thousand convicted of violent crimes. One in ten of them was Jamaican.

It is difficult, in many cases, to enforce immigration decisions by removing the appellant. If an appellant is to be removed and there is no extant travel document, that appellant will be interviewed by his claimed country of nationality before a travel document is issued. The temptation to lie, for example inventing a village from which he claimed to have come, is obvious. The foreign embassy will then, with relief, conclude that this appellant is not Chinese, or whatever, after all and refuse to issue a travel document to take him back. Many appellants deliberately destroy their travel documents and invent another country of nationality. Home Office officials trawl their records and use the European database to try to ascertain the appellant's nationality while the appellant is kept in custody and warned he will stay there unless he cooperates. Eventually, however, he is granted bail as removal 'is not imminent' and of course he absconds. Removal is not easy.

There are no clear statistics to show how many illegal immigrants are actually removed or deported against their will. It is assumed that the figure is about 4,000. Recent statistics produced under a Freedom of Information Request revealed that planes are chartered by the Home Office at vast expense; in 2015 a single Moroccan national was removed on a plane. In September 2014 twenty-nine Afghans, accompanied by seventy staff, were sent back on a plane that could seat 265 passengers. In the eighteen months leading up to June 2015 the Home Office spent £14 million on chartered flights. The Home Office is damned if it does and damned if it doesn't. It tries to remove people and then gets criticised for the cost. Some appellants return to their country of origin voluntarily with £4,000 each from the UK government to resume their previous life. It is not known how many of these then return to the UK to start the asylum process all over again. In 2014, 37,000 were removed but most were voluntary returns funded by the taxpayer.

Not so long ago the Home Office had a fast track procedure intended for manifestly unworthy appeals where the appellant would be placed in custody. The appeal would be heard in court and if the appeal was dismissed, as it usually was, there was an expedited appeal system from the immigration judge. If that also failed, the appellant would be put on a plane.

The fast track procedure was designed for cases that were easily discredited. But the Home Office then became, as it were, greedy, and started slotting Afghan and Iraqi appeals into this procedure. The Court of Appeal found in 2015 that the procedure was unlawful as too little time was given for an appellant to assemble the case. If the Home Office had stuck to the original simple procedure, with its successful removal rate, it may not have been banned.

An example showing the consequences of a failure to remove concerned an African lady who claimed to be at risk in an appeal before me. When it was pointed out to her by the Home Office barrister that she said she supported a venal dictator instead of the opposition – she got her story wrong – she screamed and appeared to have an epileptic fit, writhing around on the floor of the courtroom. I played it seriously and called for the first aiders and an ambulance which arrived in five minutes. The paramedic walked in and I asked him whether the appellant was genuine and, if so, should she go to hospital. He replied that he would apply the 'bolt test'. This involved placing the thumb firmly on a specific part of the back. If she was genuinely unconscious nothing would happen; if she was faking she would sit bolt upright. Needless to say she sat bolt upright. The paramedic said, 'She is faking judge' and walked out. I approached the lady and said, 'Madam I am informed you are faking. So I would like to proceed with your appeal if you do not mind.' She squealed, got up and ran out of court. She lost her appeal. Six years later a colleague from Bradford phoned to tell me that she was back for another appeal but this time on human rights only. Meanwhile she had had a child. I could not talk about it but just advised him to do his duty. She lost again.

This lack of enforcement by the Home Office was very frustrating. Indeed it called into question the purpose and existence of the tribunal itself, except for one point. I recognised that if a lying appellant lost, the Home Office was unlikely to do anything, often for reasons of incompetence or sometimes because the real country of nationality could not be established. But the tribunal was essential in protecting the rights of the tortured, frightened and genuine. Good could come of it.

It was also frustrating when we informed the Home Office of apparent rackets and the Home Office apparently did nothing. At one time we noticed a tranche of appellants from Sri Lanka who had all received visas to the UK to visit their family or to study from the High Commission in Colombo by using agents. The applications were made on the papers without any interview and a visa was granted. As soon as they arrived at Heathrow they claimed asylum. There had never been any family or college. I emailed the head of the UK Borders that either there was incompetence or criminal activity in Colombo and recommended an inspection. I received a poorly drafted email reply repeating the mantra that there are robust procedures in place and so on. There was no mention of

Sri Lanka. I wrote again demanding a reply from the man himself, not from a clerk with poor English. I then received another email, rather better drafted but still unlikely to have even been seen by the Head of UK Borders. There was still no mention of Colombo or Sri Lanka or an inspection. I gave up. The apparent lack of interest in enforcement by some officials was obvious.

I recognise the UK Border Agency is overwhelmed and morale is low but that cannot excuse incompetence. For example, in 2006 some junior Home Office official opened a rusty lock in some Home Office warehouse to find 450,000 files. They went back ten years and consisted of applications which had found themselves in the 'too-difficult in-tray' at the Home Office. They called them 'legacy cases' as though it was something to be welcomed. Officials then began to wade through these files. Most people had either disappeared or were settled here. Some applications were contested.

I had one such legacy case of a Sri Lankan man who had been here for ten years, had a shop, forty letters of support and kids born here doing well at school. In short, he was a pillar of the community. I told the Home Office barrister at a short hearing that I was not in the business of wrecking family lives; that it was all too late and so the appeal would be allowed on Article 8 Human Rights grounds. The Home Office did not appeal.

Home Office inefficiency was also revealed when Tony McNulty, the then Home Office immigration minister, forecast that just 13,000 migrants from new accession states would arrive in the first year. But 200,000 Poles arrived in that time plus many more from other accession states. Mr McNulty is no longer an MP.

22

WHY IMMIGRATION CONTROL?

Some ask why there should be any immigration control at all. As a broad principle it must be recognised that this country needs immigrants to bring their skills and diversity to our life. Look at the contributions to our national life of Huguenots, although Admiral Le Fanu was not forgiven by some for abolishing the daily 'tot' of rum in the Royal Navy, the Irish, Ugandan Asians and above all the Jews.

Immigration can be the life blood of a nation state but we must also have immigration control. The statistics are revealing. The government recognises that over 300,000 more enter the UK each year than leave it. Over 600,000 people entered the UK last year but that ignores illegal immigration because, by its nature, illegal immigration cannot be quantified. It is estimated that there are over one million illegal immigrants in the UK. There are 1.9 million EU workers here. Many of the new migrants are Muslim. There is nothing intrinsically wrong with that but they must be helped to integrate into our society with mutual respect. Separation does not do them any good and causes suspicion from the rest of the population. Separation, often self-induced, encourages a victim mentality.

When Lord Falconer was Lord Chancellor, his officials, showing admirable foresight, organised an 'interfaith conference' in Oxford. He kindly attended but only three judges turned up including me. Many other officials attended. There were talks from the Anglican Bishop of Oxford, a Catholic Dominican and a Rabbi. With respect to them their speeches were worthy but predictable; arguing that we believed in one God and must live with each other with charity, love and tolerance. Then the Head of Islamic Studies at Oxford spoke. He said he did not know why he was there at all. He showed two slides which purported to show that Muslims were in lower social groups and faced greater unemployment. He said they were not integrated and were therefore victims. Everyone else present was embarrassed, did not know where to look and was too polite to question the speaker that one reason for the lack of integration was a deliberate policy of separation from the rest of society, by some Muslims, as the rest of us were deemed 'infidels'.

The speaker left and did not even stay for lunch. It was all terribly sad. There was no chance to ask him what he would like to see done about this perceived unfairness. All of us wanted to address this problem and help. Much more effort needs to be taken to alter this mindset and indeed much good local work is going on in places like Dewsbury to meet in interfaith forums for mutual respect reasons. I attend one such group in Putney, where we actually pray together. All the Muslims I know were horrified by the violence in Tunisia and Paris in 2015; it was not done in their name.

As part of its duty of immigration control, the Home Office has to be far more vigilant in monitoring the imported Imams sponsored by individual mosques. Many are holy scholars but those from rural Pakistan who do not speak English can be so damaging if they preach hatred to the young and gullible. The internet must also be far more tightly controlled to get the service providers to close down propaganda from Isis and others. This can be done by threatening legal sanctions such as huge fines if they fail to comply.

The Home Office must control our borders. Some say that it does not adequately do so as our borders are too porous. The Home Office does seem at times slow to react to obvious abuses. I know that in some cases migrants will go to Ireland and then smuggle themselves into Northern Ireland and fly from Belfast to Heathrow on an internal flight within the UK where there were no proper checks at Heathrow on arrival. An alternative would be to go to southern Ireland and then take some form of ferry to an obscure port on the west coast of Scotland arriving at ten o'clock at night where there were no police, immigration officers or customs officers. These people would then get a train down to London and disappear. I pointed this out to Home Office officials but my letter was not even acknowledged.

It took the Home Office ages to recognise that the working holidaymaker scheme, which allowed individuals to work in the UK for up to one year and then have a year's holiday was being abused on a large scale. Most of these applicants received their visas and then disappeared into the work force, working full-time and stayed on illegally after the two years was up. Even the Home Office eventually realised what was going on and cancelled the scheme. Much more vigilance on obvious abuses needs to be policy.

Sometimes inadequacy of immigration control is starkly revealed on television. To look at the Sky programme on UK Border Control can be distressingly revealing. The worst case I saw highlighted by that programme involved a tall Nigerian gentleman with a goatee beard who turned up asking for admission and said that he was only aged fifteen. He must have been in his thirties. He was asked some obvious questions about when he was at school and when he was born. He got the dates all wrong and with some hilarity he was told he was going to be returned to Nigeria. He then tried unsuccessfully to shed tears and said that he should not be returned to Nigeria because he had come from Port Harcourt and was worried about some local official. He added, without evidence, that his parents had been killed. His credibility was shot through by the lies he told about his age. Then an obliging immigration officer asked him whether he would like to claim asylum. The appellant said he had not heard of this but when it was explained he thought that would be rather a good idea. So he was finger printed and released into the UK and told to report to Croydon Immigration Centre in two days' time to make a statement supporting his claim for asylum. The commentary dryly reported that he had absconded; all one actually needs to do to enter the UK is to turn up aged thirty-two, say that you are fifteen and that you are worried that you might be beaten up by a local official if you were sent back to the country from whence you came, secure temporary admission to go to Croydon and vanish. This is not effective immigration control at all. In fact, it undermines proper border security.

23

THE PLIGHT OF MIGRANTS

Much of the world is in turmoil. The number of people forcibly displaced at the end of 2014 had risen to fifty-nine million compared to fifty-one million a year earlier. Almost half of the world's refugees are children. Many of them have lost homes and relatives and witnessed unspeakable violence. Isis will stop at nothing, even the beheading of children. Christians are targeted all over the Middle East. In 2003 there were 1.5 million Christians in Syria; today there are fewer than 150,000. And there is much more to it than those affected in the Middle East.

In South Sudan more than two million people have been displaced and over half a million of them are seeking refuge in neighbouring countries. Humanitarian needs are at critical levels. Homes and belongings have been looted or burned. In the Democratic Republic of Congo there are thousands of refugees. Palestinians are brought up in real squalor in the West Bank and the Gaza Strip, with seemingly little hope of a job or peaceful life. The Palestinians should, I respectfully suggest, be given their own state and part of the deal would be that they recognise that Israel has the right to exist and prosper. In Burundi at least 180,000 people have fled the country within the last year in fear of violence. In Eritrea there is a practice of national service for many years at virtually no wages at all. Many people have fled to try to avoid this. Indeed ten per cent of the entire population has left in the last two years. Yet the EU gave Eritrea $300 million last year. Where did the money go?

Then, of course, there is the on-going civil war in Syria which has now led to four million people seeking sanctuary in other countries. A further eight million are internally displaced. There is a similar problem in Iraq. In Afghanistan the Taliban are advancing again. In Pakistan the communal and political violence means even its cricket team cannot play Test matches at home. The UK has given £405 million to Pakistan in a year and yet, in places, mobs kill Christians and burn their churches as the security forces stand by. In many Muslim countries, such as Iran, converting to Christianity can result in a death sentence. In the last year alone one million migrants have entered Europe. This will continue.

Disturbingly, the permanent secretary of the FCO recently said in evidence to a Select Committee of The House of Commons that human rights were not one of its top priorities. At least he was honest! Just about the only politician speaking up about this Christian persecution is Lord Alton of Liverpool. The Archbishop of Canterbury has also bravely become involved. Why does the government adopt such a low profile on this? Is the pursuit of commercial deals and petrodollars all that matters? I hope that in the margins of all these commercial meetings some influence is tactfully brought to bear, without a loss of face. It should not all be left to Jeremy Corbyn.

The world is indeed an unhappy place and with a good lawyer it is possible for a person from many of these places to claim asylum in the UK. These people could number many millions. So what can be done? It is not for me to dictate any solution or dictate policy, just to make suggestions with proper humility but based on experience.

We must show compassion to those who are desperate and genuine. But to declare an open door policy would invite economic migrants with no genuine refugee case at all. A further problem, which has largely gone unnoticed, is that if a nation such as Germany takes one million migrants and then decides out of compassion to make them German citizens, all of these people – and their families – can migrate to the UK under the free movement rules of the European Union. Indeed, I know of one such case where a Somali family with fifteen children and an uncle and an aunt went to the Netherlands and said they really wished to go to England. The Dutch authorities swiftly gave them Dutch citizenship on the condition that they caught the ferry to the UK. This is far from the only instance of such things happening. It could be argued the free movement across the continental EU through the Schengen Agreement enables migrants to cross frontiers and cherry pick which country they wish to go to based on social security benefits, housing, education, health and finance.

Our government, to its great credit, is the second highest international donor for the establishment and running of civilised refugee camps. Schools, hospitals and food banks are available in those camps but hygiene remains a problem and there is nothing for the migrants to do there as there are no jobs. We must also recognise that some other countries, who have taken in millions of migrants are desperate for help. These include Jordan, Lebanon and Turkey. We ignore them at our peril.

Individual people in the UK must be allowed to take in genuine refugees rather like fostering a child, if they can demonstrate they can afford to do so. Thousands of people have offered to put up Syrian refugees in their own homes but have been deterred by bureaucracy, health and safety and not being properly registered or inspected. On the other hand, although it is a wonderfully kind act to take in an asylum seeker from Syria, how is that kind host to know for certain that the refugee really does come from Syria and is a genuine refugee. The dilemma is difficult.

I have often been asked what the solution is to the vast migration from Africa and the Middle East into Europe. It is a problem caused by the conflicts and human rights abuses across that part of the world. There are, and will continue to be, conflicts over raw materials like in South Sudan and increasing water shortages from global warming. These problems will get worse.

Recently a group of retired judges and active lawyers published an open letter criticising the government by submitting that the decision to admit 20,000 refugees in the next five years was inadequate. Although such people are entitled to their views, as everyone else is, it may be suggested that such an intervention was unwise. It is very easy to climb on to the compassionate moral high ground and gaze down on the unworthy below. Indeed that action may attract ridicule as it did in the newspapers; after all, some of these people would not witness migrants in the street next to their house in leafy Surrey. They would not have to queue behind Somalis in the NHS for their operation for their hernia or piles operations as they have private health insurance. With their children at private schools, they would not have to worry about the local comprehensive trying to cope with thirty foreign languages. There is no easy answer; it is for the government, as elected representatives of the nation, to determine policy.

Clearly the numbers of people drowning in the sea from Libya and from Turkey cannot be allowed to continue. The manner in which some of the immigrants have been treated by being hounded from one border to another is also distressing. Razor wire never looks nice, especially when it keeps children out. We are a party to the Refugee Convention and we also apply human rights in the UK. We should continue to welcome genuine refugees.

I can only suggest some of the issues that must be considered. We should be proud that we continue to receive genuine refugees but there has to be a rigorous selection programme. As I have seen myself, many people before the immigration tribunal pretend to be from a country which they have not even visited. Those claiming to be Syrians may not be Syrians at all. They have false documents and they have learned their lines after careful coaching; they are young men from North Africa looking for a better life. There is nothing inherently wrong in being an economic migrant to try to better oneself. But they are not refugees. Although compassion is to be applauded it seems that the policy is to select the injured and ill from camps, some of whom need prolonged hospital treatment.

The government has to consider the burden on this country as a whole, balanced with compassion for the desperate. Migrants should be treated fairly and considerately. It may well be that we should take in more of these poor, distressed people but ensure they are evenly spread around the country. The problem is that once allowed in, people tend to gravitate to London or to conurbations populated almost entirely by immigrants. If dispersed they do not stand still. It will be interesting to study how many of the first tranche of Syrian refugees stay in Glasgow where they are being relocated and how soon they take the train to London.

Only the government knows the likely requirement for decent accommodation, but let it be said unequivocally that this is certainly not some awful pit with five to a bedroom provided by an unscrupulous landlord. Housing benefit must be paid by the local authorities. Then there are other issues such as health and education and the extent to which we can help refugees with these matters. These are legitimate considerations for the government, which is concerned not only with the financial implications for the taxpayer but also the welfare of the immigrants themselves and those who are already lawfully here.

In terms of numbers, it may be felt that 20,000 over five years is too low. After all, we took in 50,000 Ugandan Asians in one year and they have significantly contributed to our society. It may be that the government, after analysing the full cost implications, could increase the number of refugees a year to 30,000 over five years. The policy of taking in refugees in annual batches is not to be sneered at as it allows the government to assess how the process of integration is working year by year. With the distressing sexual assaults Germany, Finland, Denmark and Sweden, there is something to be said for the policy of staged entry year by year. This gives us time to study the impact and the success or failure of the integration of such migrants.

It must be recognised that if the government puts a ceiling on the numbers, say 30,000, that will not stop people gaining entry here through, as some have described it, our own porous borders. Calais and all its problems would remain. A cap on immigration numbers would be breached. The numerical difference between those who arrive and those who leave would become far greater.

The crowds amassing in Calais present real moral dilemmas. These people, if genuine asylum seekers should not really be there at all as they should have claimed asylum in the first safe country they entered. Most are there primarily because they wish to get to the UK. But the squalor is deplorable. I do not criticise the charities who work there. They have even distributed blankets supplied by Pam and me! It seems that the problem is slowly being moved elsewhere; the security is so tight that few can get through.

I feel that genuine unaccompanied minors with close relatives abiding legally in the UK should be allowed in. But the Home Office would have to raise its game. Are those identified really unaccompanied minors or are their parents nearby, hoping to follow the child in when the child has been given entry? Are they minors at all? There were many appeals like that, with twenty-two-year-olds pretending to be seventeen. If a poor child is allegedly an orphan from Syria, who got them to the camp? Were they close relatives? But if the unaccompanied minor is genuinely an orphan, lonely, young, destitute and frightened we should do more to help them. Staying in the camp may lead to assault, sexual exploitation and trafficking. These are not easy issues. We cannot just ignore these heartrending cases and walk by on the other side.

The ultimate solution, it may be thought, is to try to prevent people fleeing their homeland in the first place by assisting these countries in their economic and health provisions and reducing corruption. Corruption is a huge problem; as much as $2 billion destined for the Nigerian army to fight Boko Haram has allegedly been siphoned off by corrupt officials. It may well be that part of our overseas aid budget should be deployed to friendly countries by offering them considerable financial support in building schools, hospitals and roads on the condition that civilised and well-kept camps are prepared. In this way people fleeing persecution in Africa can go from one African country to another and be safe and well looked after without a risky sea journey until the unrest in their home country dissipates. Jordan must be a prime candidate for such help owing to the strong ties between it and the UK.

To reduce the distressing deaths in boats it may be thought that effective action should be taken against people smugglers, including targeted military action. The current military action may be thought not nearly ruthless enough. Where has the Turkish coastguard been while so many overcrowded boats leave Turkey for Greece? How many people smugglers driving the overloaded boats have been arrested and prosecuted on arrival?

It may be felt that refugees should be selected, after application, to come here directly from camps. This would avoid the distressing sea journeys where so many drown. In some cases a claim for asylum may be made from those camps and not limited to those who reach the UK only. This would require a change in the law.

Potential migrants must also be checked for signs of radicalism which can poison the minds of young and decent Muslims here already. It is madness to offer such people refugee status in the UK. The security services are hard pressed enough already without the addition of more radicalised people, admitted owing to inadequate checks.

It is not for me to pontificate on a possible solution to the problem of radical Islam and Isis but I do have experience in Whitehall working with ministers, naval and military experience and knowledge gained by negotiating treaties and international agreements in numerous foreign countries. Above all I have worked as a judge dealing with refugees or alleged refugees from all over the world.

There must be an effective campaign to prevent radicalisation from certain mosques and from the internet. Some radicals in this country have argued that even to try to prevent radicalism is to demonstrate prejudice against Muslims. This is clearly wrong as such action protects Muslims themselves. Suicide bombs kill everyone nearby without distinction. There was a disturbing documentary late in 2015 on Channel 4 where a brave, young veiled female Muslim reporter infiltrated a group in Walthamstow to record the female lecturers advising Muslims not to obey the law or legislation or take part in democracy as the only law that mattered and should be applied here was Sharia Law. There really must be much more done to counter this damaging incitement.

Some of the migrants have been filmed on German trains not thanking Allah for saving them but calling for the Caliphate. The far greater birth rate among Muslims and the declining birth rate among indigenous Europeans does frighten some. It should not be so if fair integration can be achieved.

There would also need to be checks on whether these migrants have families who would try to follow through settlement schemes. Many unaccompanied minors are dumped at Heathrow and Gatwick each year. They are allowed to stay until they are adults. Very often they are allowed to stay permanently. Indeed, I had several Afghan cases where by the age of eighteen the appellant had learned fluent English and was qualified in a trade and, in effect, very well settled. The Home Office understandably wanted that Afghan to return and contribute to the development of his own country, applying the skills learned here. They sometimes win their appeals on human rights grounds as they have many friends and have made a life here in the few years after they arrived. I have allowed the appeals of a few like that on human rights grounds as I recognised that they could make a real contribution in the UK and returning them to Afghanistan would be unfairly harsh. But when they become settled here, sometimes the family suddenly emerges from the shadows seeking shelter; fair immigration control is not easy.

More controversially, the refugees once identified in the camps may need to be inspected for health reasons. Those who reject this approach will have to concede that the NHS is not so much a

National Health Service as a World Health Service funded by UK taxpayers. An HIV patient costs £25,000 a year in drugs alone. After taking into account housing and benefit costs, the cost of an HIV sufferer can reach £100,000 a year per person for life. It is not difficult to be very sympathetic to such HIV sufferers. I had several cases where Zimbabwean wives had been infected by their husbands. But is the UK going to provide a World Health Service?

It may be concluded that the UK cannot afford to have more mass immigration. There is particular pressure on schools, housing and the health service but this is nothing to do with colour or race. I have been to my local Specsavers and been brilliantly looked after by a Pakistani Muslim female optician. My surgeon comes from South Africa. I am served in the Post Office and shops by people from the Indian sub-continent, working fifteen hours a day. There are brilliant professors and scientists here from India and elsewhere. Some of the cleverest people I have worked with were Chinese from Hong Kong. Having worked around the world when I was involved in the Hong Kong handover I have learned to appreciate other countries' history, culture and beliefs and to respect them. Such appreciation was an essential tool in the making of an immigration judge.

There is nothing wrong in being a diverse country. It should be celebrated provided that the people from other cultures can be absorbed and integrated into our rules, laws and traditions and make a contribution to society here. Still, after the uncontrolled sexual violence in Cologne and other German cities on New Year's Eve 2015 by many claiming to be refugees, a code of conduct like that of Finland and Sweden ought to be provided to refugees and migrants on local laws, customs and traditions emphasising the need to respect each other and especially young women. If such organised and cynical violence persists with utterly inadequate action from the police, sympathy for the plight of genuine refuges will soon dissipate. Genuine refugees will then be tarnished with the conduct of others. Razor wire across borders will soon follow.

The NHS relies on cheerful and competent Filipina nurses. How many times are the leading surgeons interviewed on TV seen to come from Iraq? It is sad that there are ghettos of people from different countries who all dress differently, do not speak English and do not understand our way of life, nor want to. Multi-culturalism in this country has not worked. I once had a Bangladeshi female witness before me. She had been in the UK for seventeen years, was a British citizen but could not even say 'good morning' in English. I told her that we all missed out. We could not talk to her about her own culture and family values.

We should all live together happily and be fully integrated with each other contributing to our mutual and joint welfare and happiness. As the Queen said in her Christmas message in 2015, we must learn to love one another. This is a sentiment echoed by the Gospel of John in the New Testament: 'As long as we love one another, God will live in us.' This should be the starting point for Christians, Jews and Muslims who all believe in their own one true God. Still, there is a finite number of refugees the UK can absorb. As Lord Green has observed, we should not be put in a position where we have to build three cities the size of Birmingham in the next ten years. Many immigrants themselves do not want more to arrive.

The new government Investigatory Powers Bill needs to be expedited. The government must listen to its own security adviser, the brilliant and multi-lingual David Anderson, QC. His Report *A Question of Trust* on safeguarding by judicial scrutiny of interception of communications should be applied.

As for the wider political problem, it is very tempting for a prime minister to send in the bombers to bomb from 30,000 feet or even to send in the troops. Tony Blair loved his pep talks to the troops in his shirt sleeves, a man of action being seen to be doing something. Jeremy Corbyn again is calling for caution. He is not always wrong.

But he may not be familiar with St Thomas Aquinas's doctrine of a 'just war'. St Thomas held that a 'just war' may be waged by a properly instituted authority such as a state; it must be waged for a good and just purpose, not selfish gain. As such, violence must be proportionate and peace must be the central motive even amid the carnage of violence. Later developments of this doctrine of the 'just war' held that war can be undertaken in self-defence and even against a tyrant before he has attacked but is expected to do so. (This is where the so called 'dodgy dossier' was applied to justify attacking Saddam Hussein in the Second Iraq War). Significantly it is also obligatory to take advantage of all options for dialogue and negotiations to try to prevent war or to bring it to an end after it has started.

Applying these principles and sending in the troops may be justified in law but probably not politically. The disaster now in Iraq and Libya and an unfolding one even in Afghanistan prohibit that. We do not want more brave military lives lost. We are already bombing Isis in Iraq and since it makes no sense to give Isis a British safe haven in Syria we are bombing there too. We must also show our support for France and Belgium in their hour of need. So bombing Isis in Syria is justified both politically and in terms of a 'just war'.

But bombing will not stop or defeat Isis on the ground. The more civilians are killed by collateral damage, the more support for Isis and its Caliphate will grow. Battle hardened boots on the ground will be needed to reduce the large land area Isis controls. The less land there is under the control of Isis, the more the claim to have a Caliphate is incredible. But where are these boots to come from? Ideally they should come from troops from the area. But Isis consists of disgruntled Sunni Muslims. Saudi Arabia and Qatar, where troops and finance to overthrow Isis should come from, are Sunni themselves and some wealthy Saudis and Qataris actually partially finance Isis. The Iraqis are divided and have been ineffective. Their well-equipped army did have a disconcerting propensity to run away leaving their kit behind when attacked by

Isis, although there are signs that with proper air support the army is becoming more effective.

That leaves Iran, a Shia country opposed to the Sunni Isis. But does the west want to leave the field to Iran with its nuclear and political ambitions? It may be that the huge Turkish army would get involved. But it may seek to exact a high price, like EU membership or a requirement that Europe takes in most of the two million refugees it has generously received. It is unlikely that the recent cumbersome agreement with Turkey to exchange migrants will work effectively in practice. Do we want to rely on the Syrian army to destroy Isis on the ground when that would mean supporting Assad who has killed thousands of his own citizens, men, women and children with barrel bombs and poisoned gas? That Syrian army is supported by daily Russian bombing raids, killing anyone opposed to Assad and many more besides. Few Russian bombs are targeted at Isis, but on the more moderate opposition to Assad, from where the West hopes a future government can be found. This is not easy. Who would be a diplomat trying to sort this out? It may be that a large multinational force under the direct authority of a UN resolution is the answer.

So bombing at this stage in both Iraq and Syria is justified in the short term to demonstrate to Isis that the world is against them and they cannot win. It will also have the effect, if properly targeted, of degrading Isis's ability to fight. At the same time ruthless efforts must be made to starve Isis of finance from oil and arms. But all this must be carefully and publically explained so that Muslims generally do not feel that they are being stigmatised and blamed.

In the meantime the civil war in Syria must be ended by close work with the Russians. With the collapse of the oil price the Russian economy cannot long afford the huge cost of its present activities, including impressive displays of cruise missiles sent over a thousand miles from ships at sea. The old adage that an enemy who attacks your enemy becomes your friend applies here, although the

Russians seem to be bombing the moderate opposition to Assad, not Isis. A deal should be struck for a ceasefire in Syria to enable talks to be held including the reluctant Americans. The aim would be for Assad to go so that the reconstruction may begin, enabling so many Syrians to return home.

The Russians must be persuaded to stop bombing civilian areas and to give a ceasefire a chance. It may have to be faced that, notwithstanding the brutality of the Assad regime, at least Assad permits women to walk alone and unmolested by religious police and Christians and other minorities to practise their religion without harassment. It may be that under the leadership of Secretary of State Kerry a deal can be made with the Russians and Assad to stop the carnage. This would mean everyone could concentrate on ridding the Middle East of Isis. Once peace is restored and after finance is received from Saudi Arabia, rebuilding can begin and migrants can return home. Assad is part of the problem and therefore must be part of the solution. Unpleasant though it is he will have to be involved in peace talks alongside his ally Russia. This is unavoidable.

But what about Isis? It is a ruthless terrorist organisation which thrives on fear and threats. It feels that it has been expanding the area of its Caliphate. But if the concerted bombing by so many countries forces Isis leaders to retreat to fortified underground bunkers with no chance of expansion or victory, some of its leaders may wish to give up and go home if some form of political face may be engineered, like more opportunities for Sunnis.

What follows is controversial. It should be recalled that the last principle of a 'just war' is to talk to try to bring peace. In order to end the Mau Mau insurgency in Kenya, officials and well trained and brave British diplomats negotiated with Kenyatta while the politicians were still calling him a terrorist. Peace broke out and Kenyatta became a respected president. In Northern Ireland unofficial and deniable talks took place with the IRA over many years to persuade them that military victory could not be obtained through the barrel of a Thompson gun or bombs in restaurants. A political solution was proposed and worked. Tony Blair's greatest triumph was the Good Friday Agreement based on effective work from Sir John Major when he too was prime minister.

All this shows that the unpleasant and nauseating fact of political life is that at some stage someone may, I emphasise may, have to talk to Isis or one of its agents. At the moment this is not possible; any such talks now would fail as Isis is not convinced that it will lose. It is a violent, blinkered and immoral organisation and highly dangerous. Much more work has to be done to defeat it in military terms. But eventually it may happen that some war weary leaders of Isis want a way out. If such talks were to happen they may be persuaded to disband. This is likely to be a fraught and lengthy process as fanatics cannot see reason but hopefully it may be assumed that among their number are realists who eventually would see an opportunity.

Any such talks may not be able to start for years and might then take many more years, as they did for the IRA. At the moment there is too much conflict. The starvation, death and destruction in the Middle East must stop. We must all learn to live together on this small planet of ours and stop trying to blow each other to bits or we are all doomed. We must try to love one another.

In order to end the European migrant crisis, peace must be made in Syria and Iraq; secret talks with Isis or its agent may help in the longer term to bring that about. A solution, easy to describe, but very difficult to implement may be a four-pronged approach; targeted bombing from the air; denial of access to oil, money and arms; UN boots on the ground; and talks perhaps hosted by the leading Sunni nation Saudi Arabia. Unless someone grips this, the fighting and terrorism, death and destruction, could go on for decades, with the risk that the USA and Russia would be drawn into conflict by some accident, like shooting down a plane or a missile going off course.

I recently visited HMS *Queen Elizabeth*, the aircraft carrier being built in Rosyth. She is so impressive with a flight deck longer than the Wembley football pitch. She and the other one, HMS *Prince of Wales*, being built are a vital contribution to our defence capability for the next fifty years when we will not need to use sandy airfields in risky Middle East locations but have our own airfield and a mobile one wherever we need it. The problem is that we need these ships and the F35 Lightning aircraft now.

What is certain is that the slaughter, mainly Muslims against other Muslims, the horrific brutality, the thousands killed and the millions displaced has got to be brought to an end. Then the myth propagated by ignorant fanatics in this country, namely that the fighting is all about the West attacking Muslims, can be shown to be the lie it is. To describe Christians in Syria and Iraq as 'crusaders' is obvious historical nonsense. The early Christians were in place long before the Prophet was born.

In these difficult and confusing times I feel we must have confidence in, and support for our prime minister, David Cameron and his FCO and intelligence advisers. Many are keen to try to score points or criticise the prime minister's judgement; I am sure he will be well judged by history. He is a man of uncommon abilities and he should be given more support and respectful recognition. Our long serving Home Secretary, Theresa May, also deserves support for her determination and commitment.

It is beyond the scope of this book to become involved in the issues surrounding EU membership. But I do remember that the Chinese in Beijing on the handover of Hong Kong issues were more impressed by a combined EU initiative than one on our own. The prime minister and his team including Edward Llewellyn and Thomas Scholar did an amazing job in getting twenty-seven heads of government in the EU to agree to most of the UK government's demands. The emergency brake on benefits will apply for seven years; there will be a reduction in child benefits payable overseas; the City was afforded further protection; ever closer political union for us is avoided. Their accomplishment must encourage other states to help reform the commission and its procedures also from within. What on earth will happen if we leave the EU, the Scots gain independence via a referendum and then wish to join the EU? Would the diminished and isolated England, Wales and Northern Ireland be able to retain the Permanent Security Council place?

Our intelligence network with European partners including the European Arrest Warrant and cooperation in NATO, badly needed after the atrocities in Paris and Brussels, must be prejudiced at least to some extent by being an outsider and leaving the EU

The real cost of leaving is worrying and it poses many, many problems. The Confederation of British Industry reckons we would lose £3,000 per household. What would the alternative be for trading with our biggest customers, countries in the EU? What influence to change from within would we lose? How many multinational companies with headquarters in London would leave? If we remain in, with influence over the commission, we may be able to establish that free movement of EU citizens is not compatible with our generous benefits regime. What would happen to the pound and the stock market if there was a Brexit?

If we stay could more be done to protect our fishing industry and agriculture? Would the French seek to withdraw from the bilateral agreement allowing our immigration officers to inspect passports at Calais and prevent those without valid travel documents from boarding ferries? Calais would then become an open door to the UK.

On the other hand annual immigration from Europe would considerably reduce if we left; Migration Watch suggests there would be up to 100,000 a year fewer. Our population could rise to eighty million in the next few years if immigration isn't controlled. It is said that the main draw for migrants from the EU coming here is not social security but the prospect of a job at far greater rates of pay. The minimum wage in the UK is six times that of Romania. So if we left they would not be able to enter so easily; we would not be bound by directives issued by the unelected Brussels European Commission, nor by the European Court of Justice. Our Parliament and courts would be sovereign. In short, we would not have to adhere to the free movement provisions for EU citizens.

Immigration is causing some of inner-city schools to deal with twenty foreign languages. We have an open door to our schools, housing and health service as for some extraordinary reason we do not enquire the immigration status of most people using such public services. If we stayed in we would be locked into weak economies like Greece, Italy and Spain, although we are not in the Euro. We are largely controlled by 30,000 unelected European Commission civil servants, where incompetence is common and interference irritating.

All that considered, my view is that we simply are not strong enough now to plough on in the world on our own. We still run a balance of payments deficit. If we left, the Americans and Chinese would listen to us far less. We would be a pimple on the shoulder of Europe. In cultural terms we would be cutting ourselves off from the beauty of the Italian Renaissance, the history of Greece and the glory of France. We would be an outsider largely ignored.

The dreamy romance of getting out to resume our place in the world as a great power again is just that: a dream harking back to past glories when half the world was red on our school atlases. Europe needs us and we need Europe. Leaving would cause the most ghastly administrative and legal chaos, especially as Scotland would want to stay in, with no certainty that all that chaos would be worthwhile in the end. We need our brightest and best to join the European Commission so that it might be reformed from within.

24

A WAY AHEAD

I am fortunate in that I never had to fight a war as my parents' generation had to. Even in twenty-two years in the RNR no one, as far as I knew, took a pot shot at me, although I think a shot was once fired at our patrol vessel. It missed. I have been employed and lived in a stable country in some comfort in England and especially in Hong Kong. However, I fear for the future, our future, unless we all collectively address the worrying issues we now face.

I have written this book to explain more clearly the many issues surrounding immigration and how it is handled. I also described my own journey leading to the immigration judiciary. Some thoughts are offered, not to impose my own opinions or be didactic but to offer a contribution. I do not pretend to be an expert but a humble retired judge with relevant experience. I am not qualified to tell policy makers what to do or how to grapple with such complex issues.

Immigration of new people, especially young, hardworking and skilled people or people capable of becoming skilled is vital for our economic and financial future. This has long been the case. So, as I have said previously, we need immigrants but also immigration control. It may be concluded that such control in the UK is patchy at best. The emphasis in an increasingly panic-stricken Europe is to prevent immigration by defensive measure, razor wire, gunboats and insanitary camps, like the awful camp in Calais. These measures have raised uncomfortable moral issues. Do we let immigrants in and, if so, who? Or do we let young children die at sea or in camps?

My brother Peter is the CEO of a company called Fuelstock International which employs about a thousand workers in Madagascar growing crops. The company has built a school, a medical centre and made available fresh clean water for fairly paid employees. In a well-received speech at an international climate change conference in Mauritius late in 2015, he observed that climate change, migration and indeed terrorism may in some cases be linked. To address climate change we need to adapt our approach to a warming climate and its associated soil erosion and water shortages with a more international collaboration for action. The 2015 United Nations Climate Change Conference in Paris really only got the governments on our planet to recognise the problem; there was little immediate or early effective action to emerge from it.

Peter pointed out, as I have in this book, that in order to prevent the harsh consequences of mass uncontrolled migration both to the migrants themselves and Europe in particular, more action needs to be taken to persuade potential migrants to stay where they are. So firstly, where practicable, man-made disasters like wars and especially civil wars, such as that in South Sudan, must be stopped. This means more active UN troops on the ground in some places like Syria.

Aid must be carefully targeted. Funnelling tons of dollars to a corrupt country reinforces the corruption by keeping dictators in power. The money is often recycled to Switzerland. Aid must not generally be top down to the leaders but bottom up, project led and directed at those who need it with those who project manage made accountable for results after regular audits. Some more developed countries enter impoverished ones and only apparently help. The fish stocks are diminished by the fish sent back to these countries, the raw materials in less developed countries are pillaged and sent back home. A few factories may be erected but largely employ people from the home country. Profits are expatriated. All this is facilitated by commissions paid to the local leaders.

Unless climate change is addressed there are going to be more water shortages and crop failures causing violence and mass emigration from Africa. They will come to Europe. If young men see nothing but hopelessness as their future, bitterness sets in and those young men and others become increasingly vulnerable to cult-like promises of salvation, both physically and spiritually, in religious terrorist groups. The victim culture breeds resentment. So hope must be given to the poorest on our planet, with targeted and effective aid and agricultural expertise and assistance to better govern such countries. There is little point in giving such countries aid for better and fairer government if that money is siphoned, like the soil, away.

If a farmer knows he has enough to feed his family, a guaranteed supply of eggs for breakfast, he is no longer just concerned with the survival of his family. So he may start asking legitimate questions on the reasons for his poverty. He may start holding politicians to account. Local and then national democracy may be nurtured. Some corrupt dictators rejoice in the poverty of the people, as democracy may be of little interest to those who are just struggling day to day to survive. But when there is a genuine working democracy, people are less likely to engage in mass migration. This is of critical importance as Africa is expected to experience a population explosion in the next twenty years. Responsible land development in increasingly extreme climatic conditions will be vital if inevitable mass migration north into Europe is to be controlled. Population control in Africa and elsewhere will also be important; many communities give birth to far too many children who cannot be properly fed, educated, cared for and loved.

Even the poorest in many countries have occasional access to mobile phones and the internet inspiring their ambition for a better life. This ambition, fuelled by extreme poverty, must not be ignored by European politicians. If a farmer and his large family see the soil eroded, the crops fail, the cows reduced to skin and bone and weak children die, they know they have little choice but to abandon their ancestral lands and move north. But with targeted agricultural projects managed with pride by farmers, all may not yet be lost. Those farmers must not be exploited but paid a fair price for their crops. International leadership is required, untainted by corruption and mismanagement.

This may be a Utopian vision but without such aspiration deep trouble looms. In our own country defensive measures help but we have to welcome the deserving, especially those who will help in the NHS. Our law must be simplified and enforced. Abuses like FGM and sham marriages must be effectively stopped. Those lawfully here must be welcomed and expected to learn English and integrate and contribute.

From where I stand I see there is hope, but it requires work from us all; we must learn to love one another.

ACKNOWLEDGEMENTS

This book would not have been published without the wise advice of my friend from the Athenaeum, a fine literary agent, Mike Shaw. I am also so grateful to the legendary Naim Attallah and David Elliott of Quartet Books and above all James Pulford my patient editor who constantly kept me on message and stopped me from going off on frolics of my own. I am very grateful to Professor Lord Hennessy of Nympsfield for writing the Foreword. The first draft was so well typed by Sheila Hayler of Hinton Type and Josh Bryson did a magnificent job of typesetting and indexing the book. My wife Pam who is used to correcting the grammar of seven-year-olds used that skill most effectively in correcting my own! I am pleased to acknowledge all this help, but any errors are all mine.

I have been wonderfully supported throughout my marriage by Pam and our children. I rely on her so much. Richard went to the Falmouth College of Art to study Graphic Design and does building and property development work with tough Polish workers. Alexandra is a director in Springboard Bursaries which helps disadvantaged children, mainly ethnic minorities, enter top public schools with a path to a great university and a greater chance to get on in life. She went to Leeds University and then to the Sorbonne and Trieste Universities. Susie also went to Leeds University and then helped small businesses gain contracts for the London 2012 Olympics. She set up my website for this book, a task wholly beyond my capabilities. Now she is a senior assistant director at the CBI in the City, engaged to Mark Watson, a successful barrister and all round nice guy. We love the occasional FBWs (Family Bonding Weekends) on the boat, where no one can jump off and any who have problems or worries can be constructively advised and helped with love and affection.

As for me, in the words of the case of DPP v Evans I have always tried to do my 'incompetent best' to make a significant contribution in the public service, by leading organisations and teams and changing them for the better in the UK and Hong Kong. I often remarked from the bench that I was in 'the justice business.' I have always tried to be fair, just and patient, mindful of the disadvantaged, the frightened and tortured but also of those and their advisers who were playing the system by deceit. I have tried to apply the admirable ethics in the public service learned at the feet of so many distinguished judges in the Royal Courts of Justice and senior civil servants in the old and much revered Lord Chancellor's Department, where standards of the highest integrity were expected and prevailed. But I recognise I am fallible.

I have never been recognised by the state, just a Reserve Decoration from the historic and respected Royal Naval Reserve; it matters not. I have tried to apply the famous words of St Ignatius of Loyola drummed into me at Stonyhurst College fifty years ago:

> To give and not to count the cost,
> To fight and not to heed the wounds,
> To toil and not to seek for rest,
> To labour and not to ask for any reward,
> Save that of knowing that I do thy will.
> Amen

INDEX